Heart to Heart Caregiving

© 1990 E. Sandy Powell
All rights reserved.
Illustrations by Elizabeth Powell
Cover design by Patricia Bickner

Published by: Toys 'n Things Press
                  a division of Resources for Child Caring
                  450 North Syndicate Suite 5
                  St. Paul, Minnesota 55104

ISBN 0-934140-59-6
CIP 89-20496

Library of Congress Cataloging-in-Publication Data

Powell, E. Sandy.
   Heart to heart caregiving : a sourcebook of family day care activities, projects, and practical provider support / E. Sandy Powell.
      p. cm.
      ISBN 0-934140-59-6
      1. Family day care--Activity programs. I. Title.
HV841.068 1989
362.7'12'068--dc20   89-20496
                                                                 CIP

Heart to Heart Caregiving

A Sourcebook of Family Day Care Activities, Projects, and Practical Provider Support

E. Sandy Powell

Toys 'n Things Press
St. Paul, Minnesota

This book is dedicated to Gisela, Willie and Elizabeth, who have given me constant encouragement, strength and enthusiasm for my writing.

My special thanks go to all the children who have helped me try out these activities over the years, and to their parents. I also want to thank my folks, Kay and Ken, for their help with my youngest daughter while I typed and retyped the manuscript.

Contents

Introduction 9
Chapter 1: Planning 13
Chapter 2: Equipment 21
Chapter 3: Basic Activities 27
    Messy Projects 30
    Imaginative Play 39
    Engaging Activities to Have on Hand 48
    Outdoor Activities 50
Chapter 4: Expanding Your Program 53
    Heart to Heart Caregiving 54
    More Activities to Fall Back On 57
        Projects 57
        Concept Games 62
        Games to Stimulate the Intellect 65
        Sensory Awareness Games 67
Chapter 5: Rounding Out Your Program 69
    Cooking 70
    Gardening 75
    Animal Care 80
    Movement 83
    Experiment 86
    Explore 92
    Dramatics 93
        Fingerplays 93
        Songs 96
        Flannelboard Stories 100
        Play Acting 101
        Story Telling 106
    Holidays 110
Chapter 6: Taking Care of Yourself 119

Introduction

Despite the professional hardships, most of us believe in a child's right to a fun and nurturing childhood. It is for you this book is written.

I've been where you are, one isolated home day care provider in the large, unorganized group of caregivers who are honestly and heroically trying to provide quality care for our nation's "working children." Our group is diverse: licensed and loving day care moms and occasional day care dads, preschool teachers, dedicated child care center staff, baby sitters, and countless grandmas and grandpas. In-home caregivers face special challenges. We work, alone, for long hours and low pay, shouldering the responsibility for all aspects of a home business while we monitor the well-being of children in our care. We also contend with rising insurance costs and increasing scrutiny. Despite the professional hardships, most of us believe in a child's right to a fun and nurturing childhood. It is for you this book is written.

I hope my ideas and activities will help you and your children through your rainiest weeks, through the time around the full moon when everybody goes a little crazy, and through your most difficult times. I know there isn't much money for supplies or equipment, especially when you have sole responsibility for maintaining your business. I know you are as likely to have difficulties and disappointments with over-extended parents as you are to have cooperation and support. I suspect you will feel lonely at times, even when surrounded by a loving group of little ones. I hope you will find new strength from this reminder: more than five million children are being well cared for by other loving, caring providers all across the country.

Perhaps you are new at child care. You're a young mother yourself and want a playmate for your baby or you want to supplement your spouse's income. You may have trained to be a teacher, but prefer to work for yourself. Maybe you're a grandparent, aunt or uncle and your last experience with groups of young children was in the hastily organized, but desperately needed World War II day care centers. As a single parent you may want to remain at home while supporting yourself and your children. For whatever reason, you have been moved into action by the tremendous need for someone to care for your nation's children.

Whatever brings you to child care as a profession, you will start, like all of us, from a point of inexperience. During those first weeks it helps if you can go easy on yourself. Make simple plans, establish a schedule, assemble your equipment and materials so you're prepared for each day. Then, little by little, incorporate new ideas, and your confidence will grow until enjoyment replaces exhaustion. Your satisfaction will increase and your reputation will spread until you're the kind of day care with a permanent waiting list.

Rather than give you a plan or weekly schedule, the activities here are grouped according to types so that they can be adapted to your own schedule. After all, one of the advantages of providing home day care is that you work for yourself. You get to arrange what works for you and your children. If everybody has awful colds, you'll want to disband water play and hold off on singing.

The projects in this book should be used to supplement your own ideas. Just as a writer writes from her experience, a beginning caregiver will be most effective, most inspired, and most confident if she offers activities that reflect her own life experience. Each of us is

Your satisfaction will increase and your reputation will spread until you're the kind of day care with a permanent waiting list.

Introduction 11

unique, each has talents and interests to share with our children. Instead of trying to mimic how early childhood programs *should* be, begin where you already are. If you love gardening, garden with the children. If you're a collector, show the children your china horse collection, and encourage them to begin their own collections. You can help them choose less breakable items, but the special feelings will be the same. Let the children get to know you as the individual you are, and make a special effort to know each of them. Then you can broaden your program to include their interests along with yours.

Besides the activities listed in these chapters, you can find book after book of specific ideas in your local library. You may have to adapt these to your age group, or pick and choose activities that work for you. All the extras you can bring to your program will keep it interesting as time goes on. Books can be found under Dewey Decimal sections:

371	movement	736	crafts
630	gardening	745	activities for young children
636	pets	780	music
641	cooking	792	dramatics
646	sewing	680	carpentry

A project takes on life only after you've tried it up to your elbows, in your own home and in your own way.

I love living with young children. I believe it's possible to have a meaningful involvement with the children in my care and with their families. When I'm most involved, I feel alive and excited about caregiving. It is an organic process, where I listen, adapt, create, and change and it keeps me engaged with the children. The more I respond directly to each of them with what I know will meet their needs and delight their souls, the happier they are and the happier I become. Adapt these ideas to suit your style and home day care. A project takes on life only after you've tried it up to your elbows, in your own home and in your own way. Still, this business, with all its inherent demands and frustrations, can at times seem like a sack of lemons. I hope this book will in some way enable you to "make lemonade," a big tall glass for you and a round for all the children.

My heart is with you.

♡ E. Sandy Powell

"If You Have a Lemon, Make Lemonade," by Howard Gossage.

Chapter 1
Planning

By paying attention to your own strengths and weaknesses, you can set up a program that will stimulate and challenge the children.

Many of us begin as home day care providers because it's a job we can do without a lot of formal training. We can earn a living and provide a valuable service, even when our own children are still young. Often we don't attempt a planned approach to child care because we see our jobs in a limited way. Too often, we think "I'm not an early childhood specialist. There's no way I can make up a program as impressive as the large day care centers. They know what they're doing. I don't. I might do something wrong."

You don't have to offer "the latest" in early childhood curriculum. Just present your own uniquely-created activities in ways that work best for you. With even a little planning, you can design countless improvements on repetitious, unimaginative toy box play. By paying attention to your own strengths and weaknesses, you can set up a program that will stimulate and challenge the children. Of course there will be hectic times when you improvise, and those days when everyone is tired and all you can manage is to read to the children or let them play. But in general,

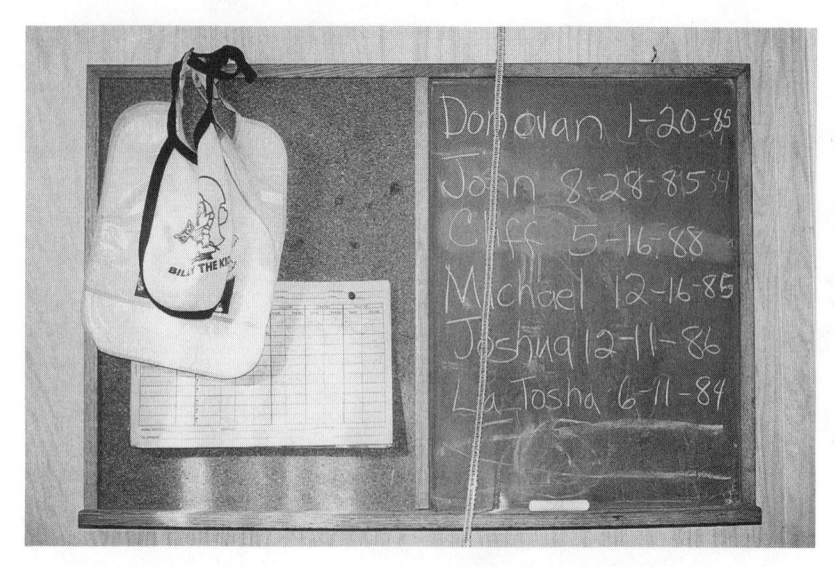

All your efforts at advance planning and organization will be rewarded. Your program will be more interesting and parents will be reassured.

a planned approach increases your effectiveness (and your enrollment).

Planning also helps you to communicate with parents. If you have thought out your program ahead of time, you'll be better able to explain what you offer to prospective families. You'll also lessen parental anxiety by speaking about your activities with enthusiasm. Take a few minutes now and then to discuss your program plans with the parents. Many long to be more included in their children's daily lives. And parent feedback is invaluable as you try to meet the children's many developmental needs. When parents leave for work confident that you have fun, enriching, age-appropriate things for the children to do, the children will be happier and more secure.

Reluctant young children can be drawn into absorbing projects with minimal planning on your part. The simplest thing, like what the children see first when they walk in the door, can affect their attitudes for the day. For example, rather than haphazardly pulling out art materials from this drawer and that, you can set out the yarns, scissors, glue, and paper in a colorful tray. Even a decorated cardboard box appeals to the children when you call it something special ("our supply tray" instead of "that box of crayons and stuff"). I often put the supply tray out on a work table just inside the back door. A clinging child can't miss it, and the parent usually encourages the child's involvement.

Some amount of time is needed each week, either before or after hours, to prepare for your next series of activities. If I'm thinking over the week's activities ahead of time, I'm more likely to dredge up some of my dormant talents and interests. I might poke around the house looking for new ideas and come across my weaving equipment. Without the children present, I can pull out the dusty old loom and figure out a way to use it with preschoolers. Or, I might think, "Say! Didn't I store my spinning wheel at the grandparents'? I'll bet the children would be able to spin." If I don't make time for planning, jot down ideas as they occur and then follow up by gathering equipment or supplies, I'm likely to become discouraged. If I try to set up the activity with the children present, thoughts like "Why bother?" will cross my mind.

Working for yourself, you can squeeze in preparation time during odd moments in the day. Just after you sweep the kitchen, you might find a few minutes to put together material scraps for a sewing project. Before bed you can take a few more minutes to outline steps in an activity that will improve its success. At the most, you'll need a weekly trip to the library or to the variety store for miscellaneous supplies.

I'm more likely to use neighbors' and relatives' talents if I've made arrangements ahead of time. Home child care offers a perfect opportunity to bridge the gap between senior citizens and little people. Older people have so much knowledge and so many skills to share. All you need to do is give them a few tips for presenting information to young children. Ask them to limit the talk to only a few minutes and to give the children hands-on objects to investigate. Teenagers have interests to share, too, like music, fashion, or world concerns. My young children once participated in the high schoolers' canned food drive. Another year our little group helped gather used items for a garage sale that raised money for world hunger, a project organized by elementary and middle school children. Would-be parents might also like the opportunity to volunteer occasionally, simply to gain experience. Remember that some planning time is needed to coordinate your helpers.

By focusing on what each child needs and planning activities to meet those needs, you will automatically elevate the quality of your care.

By focusing on what each child needs and planning activities to meet those needs, you will automatically elevate the quality of your care. For example, one child may be tentative and awkward, so you'll plan time for play on the balance beam or make up obstacle courses. Another child may have a speech problem, so you'll plan creative dramatics or puppetry. In that way the child practices communicating through the pretend character's "voice."

Finally, when you're busy observing the children and planning new activities to meet each of their needs, you're less likely to become bored. "Babysitting" can be isolating and lonely. But

Also, planning can all but eliminate discipline problems because your engaging activities will turn the children's restlessness into attentiveness.

"child caregiving" will keep your interest and vitality alive. Also, planning can all but eliminate discipline problems because your engaging activities will turn the children's restlessness into attentiveness. Home caregivers can feel proud of programs that are based on careful consideration of individual needs.

Daily Planning

Now for the fun part: What are you going to do during the day? In general, the children will be calmer and more secure if you establish a routine. I almost never hear "What can I do?" because our varied activities draw the children through each day. In fact, I've known months to go by between pleas of "Do I have to take a nap today?" The children know the answer. Right after lunch they go to the bathroom, then spread out their blankets and pillows, and get ready to sleep. You can eliminate needless, energy-draining discussions by simply sticking to a schedule. Since you work for yourself, you can always vary your routine to accommodate a special event.

Our schedule looks like this:

Morning

    Breakfast (optional, depending on arrival time)

    Open play

    Books, records, or story time

    Project

    Morning snack

    Outdoor time

Lunch

Afternoon

    Naps

    Quiet play (while the children wake at their own rates)

    Afternoon snacks

    Maybe outdoors again or a continuation of the morning play

Swing and graveyard shifts need their own schedules, determined by the ages of the children, and the number of hours they spend at day care.

I vary our schedule before the morning snack. Once I had a visitor ask, "Is this your regular routine? Drawing at nine o'clock?" The children *were* happy drawing that day, but if I tried to sit them down every morning at nine to draw, they'd soon lose interest and probably turn their creative energy into disruptiveness. Some days I might have a project prepared for those who want it. Other days I'll arrange the living room like a restaurant or a hospital for imaginative play. Or we might make puppets for dramatic play. Sometimes I scrap my plan altogether and scurry around pulling things off the shelves to enhance an idea the children thought up.

Sometimes I scrap my plan altogether and scurry around pulling things off the shelves to enhance an idea the children thought up.

It's important to offer many different activities, ones that develop fine muscle skills, communication, imagination, and large muscle development. I've noticed that if I initiate too many table activities, we become lethargic. On the other hand, if we're constantly on the go, the energy level can build until the children become hard to control. When the children lose control, someone often gets hurt. After awhile, monitoring group energy will become second nature to you. You'll know when to stay outdoors an extra half hour. You'll feel when it's the right time to draw everyone to you for a book or story. Bad weather may make it necessary for you to comfort or calm the children more. You'll learn to take in external conditions as you adjust your daily schedule to meet everyone's needs.

Weekly Planning

By mapping out your week ahead of time, you can include some enrichment activities. Maybe you'll want to do a cooking project every Tuesday morning, and on Wednesdays and Fridays you might have creative movement sessions. Each of you will determine your own rhythm for the week. If weekends are particularly wearing, maybe Monday should be a slower day, where you plan no extra activities. Or perhaps Friday is harder, so you'll need to rely on games and simple art supplies that day. Take your needs into account as you make plans for the week.

Monthly Planning

Some events you'll want to schedule only once a month. Pat yourself on the back for accomplishing one well-thought-out field trip each month. Acting out a fairy tale might be another once-a-month ritual. Or, invite a new guest every month, like your 85-year-old neighbor who's an expert at crocheting. You can always incorporate more field trips, special projects, or guests, depending upon the group's interests. By planning at least one unique event every month, you insure a minimum of extra activities throughout the year.

Committing yourself to dates on a calendar will also help you organize and prepare better.

Committing yourself to dates on a calendar will also help you organize and prepare better. As you head into each new month, you might ask yourself:

- Are there phone calls I need to make?
- What about materials? Do I have everything I need?
- Do I need to send home permission notes or explanations of a new unit we'll be exploring?
- Do I need to reserve equipment ahead of time, like the library's film strip projector?

Planning throughout the Year

Looking at the year as a whole allows you to make plans appropriate to the weather. For example, you may want to take some of your normal indoor activities outside in the summer. Or you may plan more quiet indoor activities for the long winter. Perhaps you want to establish separate units (with projects, field trips, cooking, and plant and animal study) that revolve around the seasons in your area.

As you scan the calendar year, you'll also find those long weeks between major holidays. One way to keep up your day care spirits is to declare your own holidays. Late January, for instance, can be a great time for "Teddy Bear Day." Ask yourself, "What special needs arise because of the climate or this particular group of children? How can I adapt my yearly schedule to accommodate those needs?"

It is important to supplement the children's interests with books, flannelboard stories, and film strips, etc. You won't *always* have the appropriate learning resources available because of the other demands on your time—clean toilets, fresh nap sheets, and an assortment of healthy snacks in the cupboard! I can't go to the library every night for follow-up materials, but I try to get there once a week. Being my own boss, though, allows me flexibility. Sometimes I stop at the library every few days, getting

Planning 19

a book on dinosaurs for one child, a study book on Vikings for another. Then, later in the month, I might not have time to return for a couple of weeks. Going to the library when I can is better than not going at all.

When I'm really aware of the children and their specific needs, I'm more likely to keep an eye out for supplemental materials wherever I find them. I might spot a fishing article in a magazine at my folks' and bring it home for the five-year-old whose father fishes regularly. Or I might save a stack of throw-away plastic treat cups from a party. Something about them suggests counting and sorting, which would work perfectly with dried legumes and would delight the budding counters in our group. I always try to be on the look-out for ideas and equipment to enliven our routine.

Whenever I present activities to children, I try to use an interdisciplinary, real life approach. After all, there is science in cooking, math in music, history in nature and art in everything. That's why instead of saying we're going to do an art project, I call it what it is: glueing, painting, etc. The sooner we encourage children to see the world as whole and integrated, the more whole and integrated people they will become. Unfortunately, all too soon some children will be told they have no ability in a subject and the door to that field closes to them, sometimes for good. This is not a small point; it affects the child for the rest of his or her life. I encourage all my children to paint, draw or sing, whether they are "good at it" or not.

As you get to know the individual children, you can adapt the equipment you have to meet their needs. Something you bought primarily for entertainment might be used in another context. Presented in a different way, the material could become educational, or it might even help you set ground rules for play time activities. Here's an example: When my dad first put in the 7' x 7' sandbox, I decided to introduce it with a new flannelboard story. The story was about children, a sandbox, and a monster who threw sand, put grass and rocks in the sandbox, and took all the toys away. In the story, chaos prevailed until the children taught the monster how to use the sandbox. I only told the story three or four times. The children like it, they told it to each other, and I never had a problem with sandbox play.

When I'm really aware of the children and their specific needs, I'm more likely to keep an eye out for supplemental materials wherever I might find them.

Flannelboard stories serve us well. They don't take very long to make, so you can think up a new one and have it ready the next day. Home-made books or simple board games take longer to make, but they can also be fabricated to enhance a new piece of equipment or extend an activity. Natural storytellers are truly fortunate, since an entertaining, off-the-top-of-the-head story requires little or no planning at all.

Sometimes I have trouble harnessing and scaling down my creative ideas. Children inspire such delight in living that I want to produce incredibly elaborate stories with audio/visual accompaniment, when what's needed is something simple, something that will get the job done.

I dreamed for years of making a puppet theater. Wouldn't a hand-painted wooden puppet theater with satin, tasseled curtains that opened with a draw cord be wonderful for the children? Of course it would, but I never got around to making it. One day some of the children brought their own puppets. I forced myself to cover a large cardboard box with recycled, bright-colored paper. By the next morning I had a mini-theater for their use. The cardboard box theater wasn't as charming as the one I'd envisioned, but it was there, in use. Sometimes even the over-turned piano bench has served as a puppet theater. Rather than berate yourself for all the elaborate projects you haven't created, you need to realistically assess your time and your resources, and do your best with what you have. And then enjoy it.

You may be an organized person who keeps all of your equipment, supplies and projects in a very organized fashion, but I am not. I still think I'm going to get my flannelboard stories all sorted into neat packets and filed according to subject. What a gift I could offer my families if I had these available to check out! But I get distracted, planning and taking on too much, so many of my ideas never come to life. Remember, that both styles work: being very organized or being intermittently inspired. You should feel good about the kind of equipment, activities, love, and personality that you give your children. No matter what your style, planning is the tool that can bring your style most to life.

Rather than berate yourself for all the elaborate projects you haven't created, you need to realistically assess your time and your resources, and do your best with what you have. And then enjoy it.

Chapter 2
Equipment

Finally, envision a sunlit alcove where a pair of cozy chairs face the windows to a garden and outdoor play yard. It's a day care provider's fantasy environment. Your reality, however, like mine, may be a bit different.

Imagine a cheerfully decorated house corner and a cozy reading center, where rainbow-colored pillows invite children to curl up with a book or listen to cassette tapes. Or picture a fully stocked project shelf with rows of materials available for the children, or a floor-to-ceiling storage cupboard filled with wooden puzzles, building sets, marionettes, and more. Add to this a work bench with real, child-size tools and plenty of scrap wood. Finally, envision a sunlit alcove where a pair of cozy chairs face the windows to a garden and outdoor play yard. It's a day care provider's fantasy environment. Your reality, however, like mine, may be a bit different.

At the end of this chapter you'll find an equipment list that, at first, may look like it belongs in your imaginary setting. Use the list as a guideline only. It's meant to give you a direction and an idea of what's generally needed. Don't let it overwhelm you.

I actually drew up the list from the shelves of my own playroom. (It doesn't include my daughter's toys, which she often shares with her friends.) Bear in mind, I didn't start with all this equipment. I've been accumulating trikes, toys, games, etc. for

If you're living on your day care income, you won't be able to buy everything you need or want right away.

about five years. You may not need as much equipment as I do. The children I care for range in age from six months to six years. By limiting the ages of your children, you can substantially cut down the amount of equipment you need. Of course, enrolling only certain age groups depends on how easy it is for you to get clients.

If you're living on your day care income, you won't be able to buy everything you need or want right away. So pick your equipment carefully. Remember, you'll be using it for a long time. Here are some factors you might want to consider before purchasing new equipment:

Flexibility of use

- Can three or four children play with it as happily as one?
- Does it spark the imagination, or is its intended use so specific and obvious that the children will soon get tired of it?

Durability

- If you gave this piece of equipment to your toughest five-year-old, would it last a week?

Safety

- Have you considered the ages of your children? Read *all* the labels on toys and building sets for small part warnings regarding young children. Since I care for children of all ages, I have a rule that the small-piece playthings must be used at the kitchen table or on the rug during the little one's morning nap.
- Check labels to be sure to purchase only items with non-toxic paint and stuffed toys made only with all new materials.

Variety

- Do you have something to stimulate and challenge all areas of a child's development (physical, cognitive, emotional, etc.)? It's helpful to review your entire equipment list now and then. Everyone inevitably buys from a personal preference. I notice that I tend to neglect large muscle development, because most outdoor equipment is expensive. I know I can delight the children by picking up a few puzzles, for a dollar apiece, or more colored paper and tape. Since I tend towards quieter

Try to purchase equipment that will last. Buying good equipment takes planning and careful budgeting, but it is worth it.

activities myself, I enjoy buying these kinds of things. But, if I equipped my home day care exclusively with quiet-time activities, I wouldn't meet the needs of my bouncy five-year-old. So I try to review my purchases regularly to make sure I've included all areas of child development.

Cost

- Because the park playground is only a block away, I haven't invested in large climbers. Swing sets can be very dangerous if you have a group of small children. Inevitably, someone gets knocked down or accidentally kicked in the teeth. I'm hoping to install a tire swing, but, since I have no trees large enough, I also have to build a framework to hang it on. What you'll need and what's feasible for you will depend on the ages of your children, your yard, your budget, and your personal energy.

It's possible to start with much less equipment than I have listed here. The less you have, the more creative you must be.

Remember, before you open your arms to children, those children will be with you for eight to ten hours a day. When you have positive things for them to do, you'll have an easier job and be more satisfied with your work. It's possible to start with much less equipment than I have listed here. The less you have, the more creative you need to be. One factor doesn't change: you *must* have a variety of things for the children to do.

Equipment List

Small Muscle Development
  puzzles
  building sets like Legos, Tinkertoys, Lincoln Logs
  small cars
  medium-sized cars and trucks
  wooden blocks and ramps
  construction sets
  small "round" people sets (airport, hospital, ferry, camper, garage, farm, baby)
  toy farms
  indoor pounding bench
  toy trains

Early Learning Aids
  Cuisenaire rods
  magnets
  commercial board games, or homemade
  dominoes
  floating toys
  graduated stacking toys
  alphabet puzzles
  Lotto games
  abacus
  magnetic letters and numbers
  a large stack of puzzles with varying degrees of difficulty

Exploration and Expression
  child-sized scissors, stapler, and hole punch
  protractor, rulers, and stencils for making shapes
  all sorts of drawing and painting materials
  glue and paste
  clay
  playdough makings and tools
  sewing and other craft supplies

Large Muscle Development
large balls (rubber, soft football, beach ball, etc.)
Frisbees, hula hoops and jump ropes
indoor/outdoor slide
trikes and other riding toys
sprinkler, hoses, and water toys for summer
wagon
pounding bench and real, child-sized tools
chinning bar

Imaginative Play
baby dolls, both boys and girls of several races
teddy bears
play dishes and cookware
doll blankets and beds, perhaps a high chair and stroller
doctor kit
toy clock
phones
cash register
shopping basket and play calculator
restaurant equipment (Mine was purchased at a rummage sale.)
large cardboard bricks, two sets

Other Essentials
books
records
story tapes
musical instruments (We also include rhythm sticks and bright-colored satin streamers.)
puppets and a puppet theater (A decorated cardboard box will do.)
flannelboard and story sets
sand box and sand toys (These can be measuring spoons of all sizes, ice cube trays, strainers, mixing spoons, etc., all from rummage sales.)

Chapter 3
Basic Activities

For starters, do what you love.

With so many activities to choose from, where do you begin? Which will be of the most value to the children?

For starters, do what you love. The children will be happiest if you are involved and if you are relaxed and yourself, not preoccupied with an agenda of what you "should be doing" as a day care provider. If you love to sing, sing the children through the day; work up little ditties and play games put to song. Never mind the level of your musicianship. If you sing with your heart, they'll love it.

By being your authentic self, by beginning from your world and experience, you can make up for lack of formal training. Children's most fundamental longings are few: to love and be loved, to do and be all that they can be. When they're with someone who's excited about life, who includes them and affirms their enthusiasm for everything that's new and awe-inspiring, they will grow. And when you're with fully alive children, you'll grow, too! There's so much to look forward to beyond cleaning and picking up, and the other daily drudgeries. Take time to join the children in their exciting world, where wonder and joy reside.

28   Heart to Heart Caregiving

I have a lovely memory of my children stirring big wooden spoons in their imaginary bowls as they sang along with Bing, to his rendition of "Sunshine Cake". Another of my treasured recollections is of the children riding pretend horses to Cole Porter's "Don't Fence Me In". You won't find "The Best of Bing" on any standard day care record list! Years later the children may or may not remember making sunshine cakes; they may not remember anything you do for them, for that matter. But in their hearts where it really counts, they'll know how to respond to the moment with joy and confidence.

Perhaps you like to cook. If so, include the children. Once they've learned the basics, you might ask them to share their skills in the community. Can you gather your neighbors for a noonday soup-fest cooked by the children, or take baked goods to a nursing home for tea? The children will puff up just like their bread dough when given the opportunity to shine.

Children enjoy cooking and it is a good skill for them to have. Preparing food to share makes cooking a special experience.

You can also begin by asking for help from your friends, your family, or anyone in your support group. If your aunt owns a variety store, poke around with her after hours. Look for little boxes, old lace cards, anything that might perk up an old project or inspire a new activity. Many of my day care parents teach school. They've given me stacks of used ditto paper for the children's voluminous drawings and boxes of colored scraps for their collages. Think about other sources, like what a seamstress or carpenter might share. Once our teacher/parents invited all of us to the middle school, where a llama breeder was visiting. The children got to ride along with their moms on the rattling llama cart! Later we checked out study books on pack animals.

The real life interests of adults matter to children. For instance, you might have some background in jazz or marimba. Play it for your children. I don't mean teach it. You can always designate time for those who really want to learn. I mean listen and move with the children to music that touches you. Let the children get it under their skin. Let them feel the way music can change a day. Later, they may ask for "that record" as they make a connection between the music and their activity or mood. I've had three-year-olds ask for "The Pastoral Symphony" as they put baby dolls to bed. The same is true for all interests that are uniquely yours, whether they're talents, hobbies, or special loves. The children will always benefit from your including them.

As you get to know your children, encourage them to share their family experiences with each other. Do any of their grandparents play bagpipes? Invite them to visit and play for you. Or do any of the families raise animals? From sharing like this you'll develop the group's cohesiveness and, what I call, "group myth".

So, start where you are. Bring the children along. Become aware of the children's experiences and share them in your group.

So, start where you are. Bring the children along. Become aware of the children's experiences and share them in your group. Create activities that match their developmental needs. Then, as you feel more comfortable, challenge yourself to expand into new areas, a little at a time. Remember that it takes time for all of us to grow. I have yet to take full advantage of preschool puppetry. I've made and encouraged the children to use only a very few puppets over the years. And yet I conduct lots of dance and dramatics activities. I don't know why I'm uncomfortable with acting through a puppet. One day I'll push myself to learn this art, because I know caregivers who bring great delight to children and help them develop communication skills in this way. I accept that puppetry doesn't come easily to me, and I may have to take a course to gain enough confidence to integrate puppets into my program. You, too, will have areas in which you'll need help.

When you're first starting out, you may tend to overuse some activities because you feel secure with them, but don't overdo a good thing. There is *nothing* worse than offering playdough, day after day. Even after all your careful and creative planning, be willing to let go of an idea that fizzles. Maybe you'll adapt it to another time. Or maybe it just wasn't a very good idea. We all come up with those. Doing something, trying, is better than doing nothing at all. So let your imagination go, and come up with activities unique to you, to your interests and those of your children.

The following are some basic activities that I've used to meet various developmental needs. You'll be doing hundreds more of your own before the year is out.

Messy Projects

Most preschool children love messing around with materials. The work that results is usually a by-product of the important hands-on experience. If you structure the activity for success, you can offer a wide variety of messy projects that stimulate the children's senses, their small muscle development, and their imaginations. Working parents may not have the time or patience to set up these creative activities, so it matters even more that you do.

The order in which you pass out materials is of utmost importance if you want a successful experience. Whether you use glue, paint, paste, or whatever, remember that a child will use whatever you put on the table. If you're trying to get six little ones set up to paint, helping with paint aprons, etc., and you put the paint jars on the table and turn around to get out the paper, guess what's going to happen. A one-year-old won't hesitate to get involved, and the paint could be everywhere in just one reach. A two-year-old will dip and poke, a three-year-old will try to wait but might "accidentally" spill, and so

Working parents may not have the time or patience to set up these creative activities, so it matters even more that you do.

Children must have hands-on experiences if they are to learn. Hands-on experiences are often messy, but they are worth it.

Basic Activities 31

on. Some four and five-year-olds may create more mess than the little ones if they are not gently guided. So, remember to put out the paper first, then the auxiliary items.

If you're pasting, pass out the paper, then the paper scraps, material or pictures to be pasted, and lastly set out the paste pots. You will spare the children so many "Don'ts", "Waits", and "Do it this ways" just by getting the materials in order. And as the projects go smoothly, you'll be more willing to set up messy projects again.

After a lot of trial and error, I've found it works best for me if I do the messiest projects with groups of two and three children. The others work quietly with building sets or imaginative playthings while they wait their turns. I still sometimes run back and forth between the two groups, but at least I don't have six children finished at the same time, pulling off paint aprons and washing their hands up to the elbows. In pairs, the children seem to be more involved, too, and they don't all leap up when the least attentive one finishes, as sometimes happens in a larger group.

You might want to think about how you pair up partners. Sometimes you can give the children a feeling of responsibility by letting them choose their partners. Other times you might want to use the time as a lesson in social interaction as well. Maybe two of the older boys have a conflict to work out. Putting them on the same project, both children actively expressing themselves in paint or clay, usually leads to some peacemaking dialogue. Before long their hostilities have evaporated, and the two are friends again.

Playdough is the one messy project that is engaging and predictable enough to set out for your whole group. Even one-year-olds can join right in, as long as you watch that the playdough doesn't get eaten. For other activities such as painting, pasting, and cornmeal play, I try to be sure that one-year-olds aren't paired up together. I learned the hard way what a cooperative mess they can make when two overenthusiastic toddlers began grabbing each other's paint brushes. One of them tugged at the paint container, held in the other's lap. Natch! Over it went. I had no alternative but to bathe both children. Baths are the last thing I'd want to add to a busy activity schedule!

Of course, I never would bathe a child without being sure of the parents' trust. This unfortunate morning the little ones involved happened to be my own daughter and the child of a dear friend. Nowadays, everything we do must be viewed through the eyes of parents who are wary of child molestation and abuse. I mention it

You will spare the children so many "Don'ts", "Waits", and "Do it this ways" just by getting the materials in order. And as the projects go smoothly, you'll be more willing to set up messy projects again.

Try always to see how an activity might appear to parents. After all, they have every right to know that their children are safe in our care.

here because it is a legitimate concern of parents. Try always to see how an activity might appear to parents. After all, they have every right to know that their children are safe in our care. If you plan well, share your plans with your parents, and discuss all your concerns with them, you will build trust between you and your parents and prevent misunderstandings.

Since the point of projects at this age is the experience, not the product, I strongly urge you not to make models for the children to duplicate. You can demonstrate a process like sprinkling crayon shavings on paper to be melted into "stained glass". But then your paper should be discretely set aside. The children are developing their own styles, their own affinities to color, line, and design. At their ages, trying to make specific products, even a simple one like a jack-o-lantern face, can stifle creativity. Children will attempt pumpkin faces when they are ready. Sometimes they'll ask how, in which case it's okay to show them. But demonstrate in a way that they'll still want to attempt the project for themselves. Try to resist taking over their work, placing a little more glue under this corner of a collage or cutting that edge off straight. Children learn by doing and improving on their work according to their own expectations and standards.

Every child can paint, draw, mold clay, paste, glue and do all sorts of expressive work with the endless array of materials you'll provide. I believe it is part of our job as caregivers to allow children the opportunity to create and to accept their work as it is, even when their pumpkins turn blue.

Painting

Painting with bright-colored tempera paints and big fat school brushes has appealed to every child I've known. But those precious five-year-old paintings don't appear the first time a child stands at the easel. Before children are experienced in painting you can count on paint containers being spilled and vivid primary colors being all mixed into brown.

I suggest printing for the first paint activity. Small trays, like Styrofoam meat trays, hold just enough paint so you can dip objects into them. Print painting also allows children to feel the paint, which they inevitably want to do. Toys of various shapes make good printers. I have a set of playdough cutters that double as print-makers. Toilet paper tubes make nice circle printers. You can save lots of them, so that when one tips over in the paint or gets too goopy,

Painting can be enjoyed by even the youngest children.

the children can just get another. As each child takes a turn, fresh tubes or cutters can be set out. Being last, especially when a child is old enough to know that the equipment will be well used, can be especially hard. So, try to keep your tools clean, even if they're just recycled toilet paper rolls. The children's work will be clearer, and they'll be more satisfied with the results.

Begin with a very simple project, using circles of a couple of different sizes and maybe two different colors of paint. Even with this limited equipment, each child will create his/her own unique picture. I've seen a child scrape the tube across the paper to make a large swath over all the circles. Or just one edge of the tube might be used to make slashes. The children will delight in their own variations of color and pattern, especially if you applaud their original and creative efforts.

At snack time I hold up each picture, one at a time. The children's faces beam over their work. I only allow positive comments and I try to comment on the specifics of the picture: "What an unusual shade of brown! What colors did you use?"

Next, the children graduate to poster paints and brushes. Adding a little liquid starch to the mixed colors stretches the paint and makes a glossier shine. Some people stir in soap flakes to help the paint wash out of clothes.

Water colors work best for children three and older. The process of dipping the brush in water, then wiping the brush, then dipping the brush in paint can seem very complicated for little ones. And you may waste a lot of paint, as colors can disappear in one sitting if the bush isn't wiped off well.

You can inspire lots of new ideas by varying the type of paper you use. Try construction paper, typing paper, newspaper, paper bags, tissue, and cardboard. Sometimes I cut large circles, squares, triangles, even hexagons to paint on. If you have more than one or two children, do the cutting the night before, so the children don't get squirmy waiting for you. Pinking shears make nice, jagged edges. Who has time to use them for sewing anyway? My pinking shears, like most everything else, have ended up on the kitchen counter for day care use.

Starch Painting

First, put down butcher paper or other heavy white paper for background. Next, have the children arrange cut-up or torn pieces of colored tissue on the paper. Then paint liquid starch over the tissue. It'll dry shiny and clear. Starch cleans up easier than paint, so save the starch painting for a day when your energy is low. I collect tissue paper from packages throughout the year to add to my supplies.

Glueing

There are all kinds of ways to do projects using glue. The standard technique is to assemble the paper and materials, hand the child a non-toxic bottle of glue, and then step back and let the child create. This method works well if you only have one child, or if you just won the lottery! For me it doesn't make sense. After I'd passed out six bottles of glue to my six children, I'd wind up watching a whole hour's income being poured in luscious, dribbling pools all over their papers, which would take forever, if ever, to dry. Even if I bought glue in bulk, it wouldn't work. The children love pouring glue too dearly to be able to allow them to use an entire bottle very often. Instead, I use old glue bottles in the summertime, for pouring water or sand.

For glueing, I fill the bottom of a yogurt container or cut-off glue bottle and have the children dip popsicle sticks into the glue. This involves them in yet another small muscle activity, and I can, without worrying about expenses, let all the children work as long as they want.

For glueing, I fill the bottom of a yogurt container or cut-off glue bottle and have the children dip popsicle sticks into the glue.

Besides regular glue, you can try the following:

- flour and water paste, sometimes mixed with a little food coloring
- liquid starch
- store-bought school paste
- shredded paper and water

For glue projects we've used:

- paper of all thicknesses and colors
- paper that the children have cut or that I've cut ahead of time
- cardboard bits
- small wood scraps
- magazine clippings
- Styrofoam packing material
- cotton balls (These get sticky, but the children can manage by simply dipping them in the glue and placing them directly on the paper. Good luck!)
- ribbon pieces
- old earrings and beads
- shells
- an assortment of material scraps of varying textures, patterns and colors.

The fabric scraps can give boys an opportunity to interact with materials that are traditionally feminine.

The fabric scraps can give boys an opportunity to interact with materials that are traditionally feminine. I'm always surprised to find attitudes that I had hoped died out 15 years ago still alive in my children. Five-year-old boys are often reluctant to even touch scraps of chiffon, silk, or lace, and they avoid anything pink. So now I go out of my way to present all choices to both boys and girls. Without making a big deal of it, I propose that girls can like blue best, if they want, or denim or plain, and boys can like flower prints or pastels just as well. While some children may object, "That's not a boy's color!" they still can enjoy expanding their options. One three-year-old boy I cared for just loved growing things, so I taught him the names for most of the flowers in our neighborhood. When I presented an assortment of materials for glueing, he quite naturally chose some flower prints with yellow, pink, and green taffeta backgrounds. He outstayed any of the other children and was, thankfully, oblivious to the possibility that his choices might be called girlish.

Playdough

There are many recipes for playdough. This non-cooked method is simple and surefire. Store it in seal-tight plastic containers.

Mix the following ingredients together in a large bowl:

    2 cups flour   2 Tbsp. cornstarch
    1 cup salt   1 Tbsp. oil
    1+ cup warm water

My children love the entire process of making playdough. Measuring and mixing the ingredients is a project in and of itself. Once we have made up the dough, I pass out individual pieces to knead. Pounding, punching, and squishing it lets out excess energies, soothes tempers, and calms agitated feelings. Only after the children play with it, shaping and rolling the dough into balls, worms, pancakes, etc., do I bring out the tools. If I bring them out too early, they miss that imaginative sculpting phase.

Only after the children play with it, shaping and rolling the dough into balls, worms, pancakes, etc., do I bring out the tools. If I bring them out too early, they miss that imaginative sculpting phase.

Here are some of the playdough tools we use:

- cookie cutters
- rolling pins or sections of dowels
- popsicle sticks (for cutting or poking holes)
- table knives (for a responsible, older age group)
- empty yogurt containers (for filling and making molds. I've watched the children pat out pancakes in big stacks on their upside-down containers.)
- birthday candles

Be careful about how often you use playdough. It's the one activity I've seen overused by preschool teachers. Because playdough can be saved for several weeks, teachers think they can use it every day. It's such an easy answer to the panicky thought, "What will keep them busy now?" Playdough definitely warrants a place in every caregiver's activity list, but no child wants to do the same thing every day, not even playdough.

"Me" Drawings

Cut a large piece of butcher paper for each child. Have one child at a time lie down on the paper, and trace his/her outline. Filling in the details, like buttons, belt, and facial features come later. To prevent the lengths of paper from getting all wrinkled, I stack them on the counter until I've traced everyone's outline. Once I let the children hold theirs while they waited, and in no time they were racing back and forth to make their pictures fly around or covering each other up. "Me" drawings are easiest to present if the children have already had some practice in waiting turns.

When everyone has an outline, pass out containers of crayons. You may want to ask if they're going to color in the clothes they have on or color their favorite outfit instead. Keep in mind, this life-sized picture is too big for most children to color completely in one sitting. If a child tries to be precise, he/she might get involved in the details on one sleeve but not be able to sustain enough attention or energy for the rest of the picture. You can always invite the children back to their coloring after naps or allow them to finish the pictures at home.

Staying inside the lines and being "realistic" should be our last concern when children get creatively involved.

"Me" drawings can be a wonderful opportunity for children to observe and transpose patterns from their own clothing to their pictures. But we also need to be sensitive to those children who have their own creative response to this project. I recall a child of two-and-a-half who was particularly intrigued by rainbows. She made a beautiful rainbow sweep all across the front of her picture. What a lovely statement of her positive self-image! I would have missed this little girl's expression if I'd insisted she duplicate her clothing, because she wasn't wearing rainbows that day. Staying inside the lines and being "realistic" should be our last concern when children get creatively involved.

Record Player Drawings

Cut out a stack of circles the size of your turntable. Place one circle on the record player as you would a record. By touching a marker to the paper while the turntable goes around, circles upon circles appear. Each child takes a turn making his/her own record. An assortment of markers with different-sized tips adds variety and encourages creativity. Sooner or later someone discovers a back and forth motion with the marker; then everyone has to have another turn to make "the squiggly kind."

I have a beat-up old coffee table that I move about the house to fill various needs. For cornmeal play I bring it to the kitchen.

Cornmeal

Sand is a wonderful element that has been used for ages by children at play. But what can you do if the rains keep you from your sandbox, even for months on end? Or perhaps you live in an apartment and have no sandbox. I suggest cornmeal. However, beware. I've never come across a more slippery surface than cornmeal on a kitchen floor. And no matter what precautions you take, some of the cornmeal is going to spill.

I have a beat-up old coffee table that I move about the house to fill various needs. For cornmeal play I bring it to the kitchen. I set up two child-sized chairs opposite each other at this low table. Then I put two dishpans in front of the chairs and fill each pan one-quarter to one-third full of meal. I've also used a roasting pan. A large (new and unused) plastic litter box makes an ideal work basin for cornmeal, water, or any number of activities for mixing. Occasionally, two very cooperative children have used the same pan. Most often this needs to be another two-at-a-time project, with the basins opposite each other.

You might try materials like these with the cornmeal:

- small set of farm animals and fences
- matchbox construction equipment
- funnels, measuring cups, and spoons
- miniature rake, shovel, and hoe sets
- small containers for filling and pouring, such as travel shampoo bottles.

You'll find more ways to set up cornmeal play in Chapter 4, "Expanding Your Program."

Shape Stencils

Shape stenciling is an easy, engaging activity for those odd times when you don't have the energy for a mess. Stencils can be purchased at early learning supply centers, but I find it easy enough to make them myself. From medium-weight cardboard, like the kind found on the back of writing tablets, I cut stencils of squares, rectangles, triangles, hexagons, circles, and ovoids. Depending on their age levels, children use these either as a pre-writing exercise or for drawing various combinations of pictures or designs.

Basic Activities 39

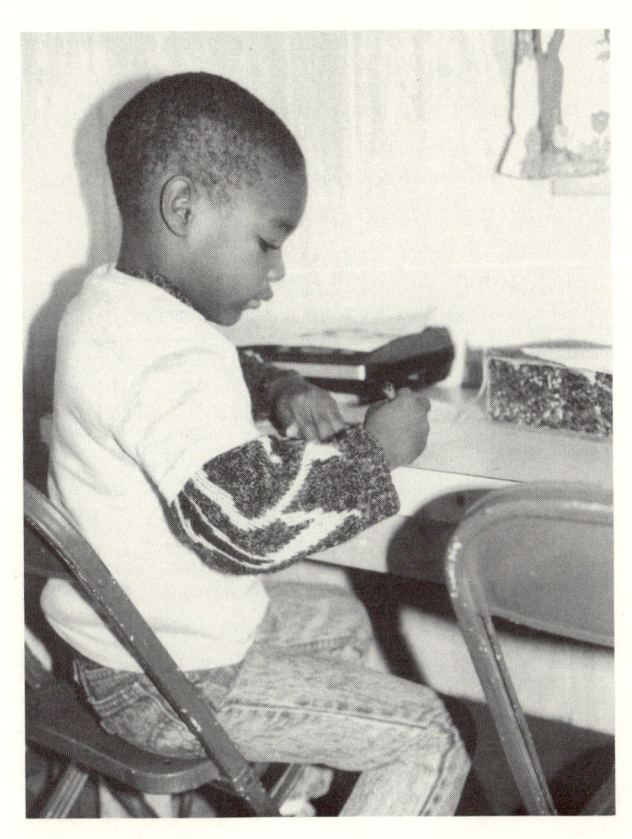

Working with pencils or crayons is the kind of activity that appeals to a variety of ages, and it's relatively mess-free.

Occasionally I get inspired in the evening and make some new stencils. Our collection includes hearts, stars, simple animals, flowers, etc. Once made, the stencils last at least a couple of years. Worn out ones can be easily replaced. As with every project, I have to watch that I don't overuse stenciling, or the children will lose interest. Sometimes changing the work setting, like drawing outside or on the front porch, will spark renewed interest in an old activity.

You'll expand on these activity ideas, creating your own list of favorite messy projects. I suggest no more than one messy activity a day to satisfy the children's creativity. Some days you'll want to do other things instead of a project, such as field trips, extended outdoor time, cooking, or inviting a guest to visit. The messy activities are easier for me in the morning, when I still have lots of oomph, and when we have the longest block of uninterrupted time. On the other hand, if you work until 5:30 or 6:00 p.m., the late afternoon might be a calm time for a messy project.

In the late afternoon, giving the children access to a self-help shelf might be soothing for them and a little easier on you. If you don't have a special shelf or can't keep it stocked because of the one-year-olds in your group, just set out the supply tray full of scissors, tape, paper, crayons, etc. Only try not to squeeze too much into one day, because children need lots of time just to play.

Imaginative Play

When I was first setting up my home day care and brimming over with plans for creative activities, I tended to place less value on the time the children spent in play. I often felt guilty if I wasn't leading an organized activity. I wanted to be giving "quality" day care. (What would I tell the parents if the children were just playing?) But I soon realized the need to balance structured activities with open-ended play.

All children, especially "working children" need time to play.

All children, especially "working children" need time to play. Their little bodies must have constructive ways to use their abundant energy. If children aren't active, like when they sit in front of T.V. for hours, their muscles don't develop. Even more alarming, if their minds aren't used and their imaginations given free reign at least sometimes, children lose their innate creative abilities. Caregivers can encourage both imagination and physical development by providing a positive environment for playtime.

Play is also the perfect arena for developing social skills. Children learn to take turns, to listen, and to assert their desires. With help, they learn to talk out their problems and to express their feelings in acceptable, understandable ways. By making time for play, caregivers nurture many parts of a child's development. We have a responsibility, though, for the kind of play we encourage. If our toy boxes are full only of guns and other toys associated with war, children will play aggressively. If, however, we've been selective, accumulating an assortment of interesting props, we can set the stage for positive, inventive, and generally peaceful playtimes.

Play is therapeutic. Children often act out their problems and feelings through play. If a family member has been ill, children seem to gravitate toward doctor and hospital play. If a mother begins to work at an office, a child may want to play home and office, assuming the various roles of family members. Open communication with the parents will help you to offer the right play equipment at the right time. For instance, chairs lined up in a row can simulate a train trip. Extra places set at a table, and pillows and blankets spread on the floor can suggest a visit to a relative. The props don't have to be elaborate. Through their imaginations, the children will recreate or make up real life concerns and then work them out in play.

The arrival of a new brother or sister always bring out a baby doll and newborn paraphernalia. And don't be surprised when the sibling throws the baby doll away. Remember, this is therapy. Echoing a child's feelings by saying, for example, "Sometimes you wish the baby was gone.") will bring about adjustment and a positive attitude sooner than reprimanding or denying his/her feelings. At times like this, a child simply needs to feel heard. Better to act out the ambivalence with friends in play than to take it out directly on the new baby.

By watching children at play, paying attention to the way they approach each other, and the issues they raise, you can gain valuable

Through imaginative play children learn how to express feelings.

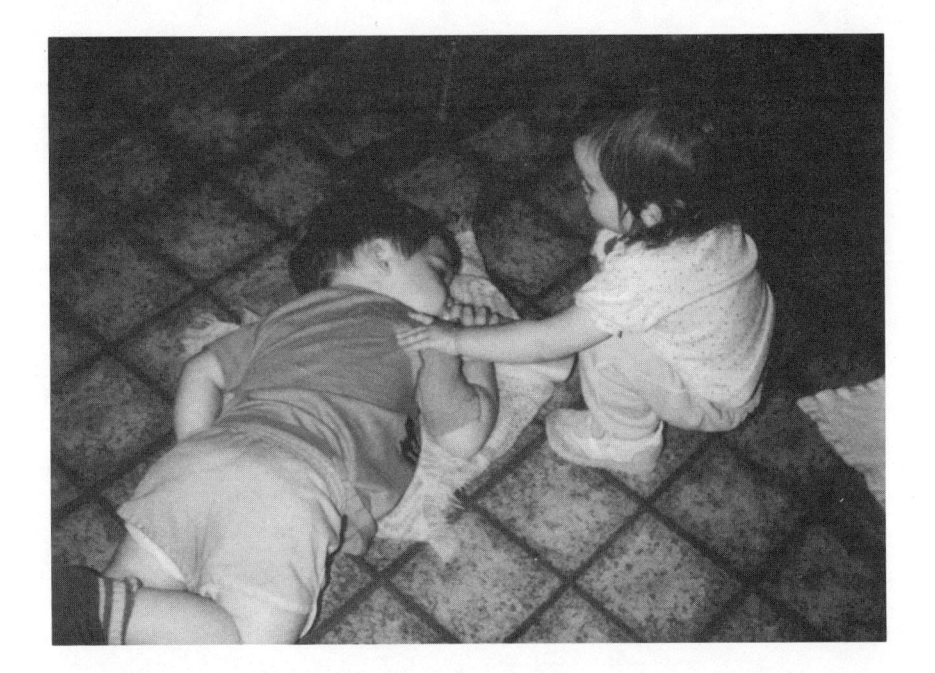

insights into their thoughts. At times, I've been almost embarrassed by the transparent quality of their play dramas. Unintentionally I eavesdrop on family affairs as the children imitate their families' dynamics. They might act out how mom feels about dad being late, how dad feels about his uncle's drinking, how the family welcomes visitors, or how the parents relate to the children. All this and more comes out in their play.

It's your job to accept these dramatizations and to allow children to examine, through play, their own family ways. It's not your place as a caregiver to attempt to restructure family relations, unless behavior at home hurts a child or other children in your care. If any real harm is being done, you must deal with the problem directly by getting the parents involved.

Nevertheless, it is your prerogative as a caregiver to enforce your own values during the time the children are with you. There is a difference between, "We don't say 'shut up' here" and judging people who do use those words. Later, with a group of children, you might explain further by saying, "Building up words feel better than words that knock us down." So, you haven't shamed an individual child, and you're free to brainstorm "building up" words with the group.

Over the years I've derived the greatest joy from just standing back and watching those magical moments as the children play happily in an environment I've helped create.

The type of guidance you offer children will be reflected in their play. If the equipment you provide is stimulating and the atmosphere is positive, the children can have endless and generally peaceful playtimes together. Over the years I've derived the greatest joy from just standing back and watching those magical moments as the children play happily in an environment I've helped create. Here are some ideas I've used to set the scene for imaginative playtime.

Playhouse

Children gravitate to house play, because it reflects real life as they know it best. Cardboard boxes, bricks, and throw pillows can make as good a playhouse as the more elaborate or expensive ones. Usually the children play the part of a mom and/or a dad who takes care of the children with child-sized dishes and cookware, small table and chairs, stove and fridge, baby beds, and perhaps a little high chair or buggy. Often the mom and/or dad goes off to work, in which case the children need a briefcase, lunch box or purse to act out the scene realistically. Sometimes a child, pretending to be mom, will stay at home for the day. Remember that in play, children have the power to remake their world in any way they choose.

Several years ago I adapted the traditional home corner to fit my group's passion for outer space. Actually, it was much like the usual home corner with individual table-like pieces, but in this case the tables had crater tops. Large wooden blocks made a space station nearby, and, as I recall, the moms and dads left for work in a rocket. By slightly redesigning the home corner, I was able to redirect the children's space-war play, without squelching their interest in outer space.

Large cardboard boxes from furniture stores make marvelous playhouses. We've enjoyed painting them, putting on a chimney, or sometimes cutting heart-shaped windows and round doors. Don't be surprised, though, if the box play never progresses past "going home," where the children crawl into the house all at once, sometimes accidentally tipping it over. To children, something about a large box invites its destruction.

We all remember making tent houses in one form or another in childhood. I've tried using card tables covered with blankets, and for something different, I discovered my fold-out couch makes a wonderful housetop. I think the discovery occurred when we were looking for missing pieces to a building set. When I pulled out the

Now that I think of it, I could make more playhouses outdoors, using little areas or enclosures where the children could act out their make-believe dramas. Last year's group simply loved the back steps for their house play.

couch, the children scurried under. From then on, the couch tent became a winter favorite. On very special days I fold out the couch half-way, put a baby bed under one end to keep it from collapsing, cover the whole thing with blankets, and, wonder of wonders, the children all play happily together inside the tent house. Usually they cart in so many household items, there's hardly room for the children!

Now that I think of it, I could make more playhouses outdoors, using little areas or enclosures where the children could act out their make-believe dramas. Last year's group simply loved the back steps for their house play. Trikes became cars going to work; anyone left at home would either "sweep the house" or stretch out on the cool steps to await the family's return.

Restaurant

One day my little ones and I were out for a walk when we passed a church rummage sale. Since I knew the people working there, I ventured inside, handing each child a nickel at the door. The children only spilled one large box of puzzle pieces as they hunted for treasures to take home.

Then we all looked through the housewares section. Together we found item after item, all for nickels and dimes, that would make good restaurant equipment: baskets like the kinds used for burgers and fries, plastic catsup and mustard containers, a plastic grinder (which became one of the best-loved toys in our house), trays,

Replaying events that have been experienced with their families are favorite dramas that children love to re-enact.

Sometimes just a few well-chosen props will inspire hours of imaginative play. An office is an easy environment to set up.

spatulas, etc. We bought as much as I could carry. During nap time I washed the equipment, and when the children awoke, they played restaurant until it was time to go home. I remember a few parents that afternoon, trying to be patient as their children coaxed them up to little tables where they were to order and eat pretend restaurant food.

A rummage sale, especially the larger church variety, is a marvelous place to outfit your store, office, or camp-out. I've thought twice, however, about frequenting them with the children. But on that particular, unplanned outing, our shopping trip was unquestionably profitable, in more ways than one.

Walkie-Talkies

Whether they are used from boat to shore (both indoors and out), trikes to porch, or kitchen to living room, walkie-talkies inspire lots of innovative group play. I don't mean the expensive store-bought sets. I'm talking about a chunk of wood that the children color and pound nail "antennas" into. Or, I think of the walkie-talkies made out of the sturdy check boxes that my bank regularly sends me. Once I saved enough to be sure I had one for each child and then dramatically brought them all out, one after another. I had enough so that the children never got to finish the "I want one!" chorus. "You have one for everybody?" they kept asking. It also helped that I had picked just the right day. If treated with specialness, a simple scrap of wood or a recycled box can bring hours of delight to these little ones. The coloring, name-inscribing, and antenna-fastening lasted just until we had functional, pretend walkie-talkies. They they were off, in play, creating the most wonderful real-life scenes, cooperating, and working out problems. Sometimes we've kept all the children's walkie-talkies at school in a set; at other times, they've taken them home that very day. The activity has been so successful that we return to walkie-talkie play every few months.

You don't need sophisticated, expensive toys to set the stage for children's play. Some store-bought sets, like doctor's kits, cash registers, etc., are worth investing in someday, because they will be played with continuously. But if you can't yet afford these, use your imagination to design other settings.

Here are some examples:

- **Store**

    empty boxes and containers as items for sale

    cash drawer and play money

    basket or cart

    baby doll to take along on a shopping trip

    small broom, mop, or duster for store cleaning

    counter for inventory

    small pad of paper and pencil for lists

- **Office**

    an old typewriter or adding machine

    dividers for filing papers

    cards or tickets

    desks and chairs

    a telephone, either pretend or real

    a "lunch room" area with tea set

- **Travel agency or airlines**

    tickets

    chairs set up like an airplane, including chairs designated for the pilot and co-pilot (Be sure that girls and boys get equal turns. Boys can be stewards, too.)

    travel brochures

    trays or cardboard box lids for an on-flight meal

    pillows

    carry-on bags

    magazines

    baby doll and bottle

- **Library**

    books, of course

    cards in books

    stamps (Bear in mind the age and responsibility of the children.)

low tables or pillows for reading

coffee table for check-out counter

- **Theater**

    tickets

    ticket booth

    chairs set up in rows

    popcorn

    sheet for a movie screen (optional)

    (The children take turns being the audience and acting out the movie.)

Imaginative play equipment can be stored in colorful stacking bins, each containing items for a particular play theme. Decorated cardboard boxes work just as well. Even labeled paper bags can get you organized. Use whatever suits your budget and your style, so that you can offer restaurant play one week, doctor or office play the next.

Responding to a theme suggested by a child can encourage hours of imaginative play.

I find that children become more involved when toys are presented by theme rather than piled haphazardly together on a shelf or in a toy box. They will ask for sets of equipment, too, sometimes needing to combine different toys to have the play unfold the way they want. "Office" and "restaurant" may need to be set up next to each other as the children imagine their parents "going to lunch". They act out the drama as a way of understanding and connecting with their working mothers and fathers.

You can also vary the play or respond to the children's spontaneous suggestions by relying almost entirely on their imaginations. You'll find a set of large cardboard bricks invaluable for this purpose. The bricks can be stacked for building houses, barns, workshops, etc. They can be used as dividing walls between play areas or made into bridges and roadways for cars, large and small. Sometimes they serve as oven, gas pump, baby beds, or doctor's table.

One use we've returned to a number of

times is the living-room-size brick boat. The children love it when we make it together and shape a nice point at the bow. Sometimes we've built a secret compartment into the stern. Our indoor slide has been added at times as an upper deck. I usually have empty toilet paper or paper towel tubes ready to use as telescopes. Sometimes we bring out the toy dishes and cocoa after a "storm". And we always take along the fishing poles, whether they're the plastic variety or just wrapping paper tubes.

While cardboard bricks are usually indoor equipment, they can be carried outside by the armload for a change in brick play during dry weather. If treated with care, the bricks will last for years.

I save everything, either for projects or play. Eventually a use arises. Empty diaper boxes first because part of our recycled equipment when I was scurrying around the house looking for suitable garages for the vans that showed up at day care that morning. I happened to come across an empty diaper box in the bathroom and remembered I had several more stacked in the basement. From then on we looked for other uses. Some of the most fascinating ideas come from the children themselves.

Over the months the diaper boxes became:

- trains
- baby beds (for dolls, teddies, and an occasional two-year-old)
- TV's
- pyramids
- cars, with wheels
- baby swings (for dolls and teddies)
- doll houses

It doesn't matter that the boxes have a previous identity. What the children see in them is what's in their minds and hearts. You'll be doing children a tremendous service when you nurture their imaginative play, and one day the good will come back to all of us: after all, our world needs people with vision!

Engaging Activities To Have on Hand

Sometime early on in my childhood, Grandma brought out her canning jars, full of garden-dried beans.

A Whole Bunch of Something

This play originated on my grandmother's rug thirty-some years ago. Our family couldn't make the long trip more than once or twice a year, so Grandma and Grandpa never accumulated many toys or games. Yet we children needed some activity during the evenings. Sometime early on in my childhood, Grandma brought out her canning jars, full of garden-dried beans.

The first time the jars were brought out, my brothers and I immediately poured all the beans into a big heap on the floor. I have a vague memory of working for hours, separating all the beans into four piles. Next, we made patterns and pictures and wound "trains" around the grown-ups in their chairs. Sometimes Grandpa taught adding and take-away with the big Mexican limas. Invariably, we'd settle into a quiet spot and trickle the beans through our fingers over and over, mesmerized by their slippery coats.

A bowl of polished agates has inspired similar enjoyment for my mom and youngest daughter, Elizabeth. They often lie on Mom's rug, feeling, sorting, and lining up agates in intricate pathways and patterns. Elizabeth has had everyone in the family pick a favorite, so the activity also includes her spotting and passing out each person's agate, which she remembers even after weeks have gone by. For home day care you might also make collections of rocks or shells to provide this fun tactile experience and to challenge the children to recall each other's favorites.

For my group of varied ages I've used a shopping bag filled with walnuts. You need to be constantly wary of young children putting small objects in their mouths, but if a little one pops a walnut in the mouth, the bulging cheek is an immediate give-away. Not taking any chances, I stay right with the youngest children. Although walnuts aren't as smooth to the touch as agates or beans, the children still delight in "a whole bunch of something." Their enthusiasm overflows when I bring out a shopping bagful, and there's no end to the baskets, pots and lids, wooden spoons, and plastic containers they drag out of the cupboards. By the time we're through, we have walnuts from one end of the kitchen floor to the other. Walnuts give us so many possibilities for fun: pouring, stirring, counting, trading, and pouring some more. I don't know if we'll ever be able to part with those nuts for baking.

A Rolled Road

In any child care setting, block building is as indispensable as good food. For variety, I sometimes roll out a long strip of two-foot wide butcher paper and tape it to the kitchen floor. Then, depending on the children's ages, one or all of us draws roads or oceans on the paper. We get out animals, trucks, even boats to enhance the block building experience. Once I had a five-year-old who was interested in Vikings. After we made a library trip to study the real thing, we built an elaborate Viking village on a butcher paper roll, complete with Viking boats made from halved plastic milk cartons.

Baby Toys

I keep a basket of baby toys on top of the fridge, the best from several years of caring for babies. You know the kind: the squeaky ones, the chewy ones, the rattles with a pleasant sound. There will be a right time, sometimes months apart, when the absolutely perfect thing for a certain child is this basket of baby toys. The toys are a treat, not an implication that the child is a baby. When I offer them by saying, "Do you want to look at the baby toys?" the child's eyes light up. Here is an acceptable time to revert to babyhood, even for just a while. So chew a little; goo a little; it's okay. All children need to touch base with their earlier years now and then, especially if they're competing with a new baby. Or, a child arising early from a nap and not quite ready to get going for the afternoon might be happy on a blanket in the kitchen, "looking at" the baby toys.

All children need to touch base with their earlier years now and then, especially if they're competing with a new baby.

Pounding Stumps

There are times when, rather than being quiet and cuddly, a child will storm through the day, smashing and crashing. I have a pounding stump on the front porch for just those times. I offer large-headed nails, about 1-1/4 inches long, and a sturdy, child-sized hammer. Once the children fill one end of the stump, I turn it over, and they fill the other. Even two-year-olds can successfully pound a nail.

Hitting a punching bag or a pile of pillows also helps children to get rid of built-up feelings. If a child is angry, aggression will come out, one way or another. Rather than stifle all that turmoil, give the child no-hurtful, physical ways to express and move through these feelings. Once the first wave of emotion is out, you can help the child verbalize what's wrong. Sometimes, when the feelings aren't specific, an acceptable physical outlet is the only real solution.

Outdoor Activities

In addition to the basic indoor activities I've outlined, children need plenty of opportunities to run, jump, and climb in unstructured outdoor play. Their large muscles and gross motor skills will develop in proportion to the amount they are used. So, take special care in creating a fun, yet safe, play yard for your children. Balance beams and chinning bars can be constructed inexpensively. Trikes, scooters, and assorted riding toys all promote balance, left/right coordination, social interaction, and unending enjoyment. These can be purchased one at a time, as you can afford them.

Your physical surroundings will dictate how freely your children can play. While a large climber with a slide, an outdoor playhouse, and pavement for riding toys (protected from cars) allow the most freedom in active play, you may not have all of these settings. If you don't, you'll have to work harder to create positive outdoor experiences, but it can be done. I use the park playground, appropriate for preschoolers, for many of our outdoor times. Often I've brought out the old wooden wagon to pull the little ones there.

If you don't yet have any of the larger pieces of equipment, and you don't have a park nearby, you'll need to invent some simple games and activities. Play in an empty yard just isn't acceptable, for you or for the children. I suggest setting up an obstacle course, at least once a week, adding variations from time to time: a hula hoop to go through, a cardboard box to jump over, a two-by-four to walk along, or a bench to crawl under. All these will challenge the children's coordination and help physical development. You can also set up bean bag tosses, basketball hoops, and ring tosses for more large muscle movement.

The children will naturally demand seasonal activities like running through sprinklers or building snow people. You can enrich summertime experiences by gathering water-pouring toys (start with old plastic shampoo bottles and dishpans). If you can, add funnels, plastic gutters for waterways, water-wheels, etc.; the more the better. Warm weather is also a good time to bring all the doll clothes outdoors. The children can scrub them in a basin, then hang them up on a clothesline. In the winter, if you're fortunate enough to have snow, encourage dressing and decorating the first snow people. On another day, you might return with safe putty knives to try your hands at snow sculpting. You can also try snow block building and assemble a house or a wall made with blocks of snow.

If you don't yet have any of the larger pieces of equipment, and you don't have a park nearby, you'll need to invent some simple games and activities. Play in an empty yard just isn't acceptable, for you or for the children.

Basic Activities 51

A busy summer morning often ends with wet or sandy shoes. Knowing that the children had fun and were very busy makes it easier to deal with messy shoes.

Warm weather is also a good time to bring all the doll clothes outdoors. The children can scrub them in a basin, then hang them up on a clothesline.

Sometimes you'll need specific outdoor activities to redirect wild energy into positive play.

Here are a few I've used:

- hopscotch, drawn with chalk or tape (Even strips of cloth laid out on the ground can make a hopscotch game.)
- chalk drawing on a sidewalk
- chalk drawing on wood ends
- relay races of all sorts, including crawling, running backwards, carrying things, balancing, etc.
- games of catch with assorted balls
- marbles (or try a variation where each child rolls a marble into a ring made of string, rather than the more competitive version.)
- roads and villages made from blocks of wood, sticks, or rocks

To nurture the children's imaginations in an outdoor setting, you might want to gather some of the following:

- sets of camping gear with flashlights, pots and pans, small tent, mats, camping mess kit, basket or box, lashed hooks or racks, pretend first aid kit
- inclined plane for rolling balls or cars
- old rowboat, or large cardboard boxes for a fleet of boats
- a gas pump or box with a hose for "filling up" trikes
- a bench or a sign for a "bus stop"
- a large furniture carton for a playhouse

One way to help create those carefree times is to give yourself permission to relive some of your childhood fun with the children in your care.

Whatever you do outdoors, keep it light and playful. Nowadays, children must adapt to their parents' working schedules, take lessons of all kinds, and strive to become accomplished in so many ways. The result is that they get less and less chance to play. One way to help create those carefree times is to give yourself permission to relive some of your childhood fun with the children in your care. When was the last time you sat on the lawn and made little stick houses? Or drove mini cars around on dirt roads? Or leaned against a mossy rock just to watch the clouds? We can all find the time now and then, and, oh, what serenity it'll bring the children!

Chapter 4
Expanding Your Program

You know, whether or not you feel inspired, that you have to have something for them to do. If you don't, the children will come up with something on their own.

Eventually there comes a day when you feel as though you've done it all. There isn't an activity you haven't tried. Still the smiling parents will arrive at 6:45 a.m. to leave you their bouncing or cranky-tired children. You know, whether or not you feel inspired, that you have to have something for them to do. If you don't, the children will come up with something on their own. Well, just remember that old-fashioned childhoods weren't without mischief.

One day this realization hit home when I returned to the living room after feeding the baby. There, before me, lay the entire contents of the adjoining playroom, piled in the middle of the floor, a mountainous task accomplished quietly with the oldest child in the lead. Of the five children, he alone did not look innocent. The "dump" took our entire crew a good thirty minutes to clean up. For the whole next week the children asked, "Can we play Garbage Dump today?" I assured the leader it had been a harmless enough activity for one morning, but I implored him to instill some reason in his friends. Our toys wouldn't last if "Dump" took hold. From that day on I knew I needed my own endless list of ideas.

In this chapter I offer more activities for the veteran child caregiver. It's a real challenge to stay motivated and inspired all the time. Even after you've established a positive, happy rapport with the children and earned the title "experienced," you still can use all the help you can get.. Perhaps then, more than ever, you have to guard against getting stale. It won't be easy, but, since you work for yourself, you can chart your own course.

Heart to Heart Caregiving

The most helpful ideas are those that can be adapted to various ages, group sizes, length of activity time, individual children, etc. Sylvia Ashton Warner, a teacher of New Zealand Maori Indians says to begin with the child and the moment. Her "organic" learning comes as the adult hears and responds to the individual child, heart to heart. For example, I know I can excite, inspire, and teach a three-year-old boy I care for by showing him a new flower in bloom or by letting him browse through a new seed catalog. We walk around the yard together, naming shrubs and flowers. But the most fun comes for him when we actually grow things. He's so eager and so appreciative of every new gardening "lesson".

Yet each child is different. Another will respond to mechanics of all sorts, so I get study books on machines and motors, or we just plain "tinker" together. Or another child has a fanciful imagination, so we write stories, sing, and dance. Rather than teach a set curricu-

Children need the chance to develop real life skills. Without this chance, they may never get to develop their personal interests.

As you combine the children's unique interests, blending them with your own, a "group myth" can emerge. I call it "myth," because the individual activities often co-mingle in an almost surreal way. No two groups have the same myth.

lum, in home day care you can create as you go along, teaching and responding from the heart. Of course, the children also benefit from being involved in what each of the others likes to do.

As you combine the children's unique interests, blending them with your own, a "group myth" can emerge. I call it "myth," because the individual activities often co-mingle in an almost surreal way. No two groups have the same myth. One group's favorite activity may be Teddy Bear space travel, while another group doesn't pay much attention to stuffed animals but is intrigued with insects or caves.

Sometimes, because of a caregiver's ability to spin a yarn, story characters become woven into the group's experience. For example, dinosaurs and unicorns often fascinate young children. The way the children relate to these awesome creatures determines whether they become a part of the group myth: Do the children "feed" the unicorns in the back corner of the play yard? Does the caregiver make up unicorn games? Do they make an ongoing pretend picture journal of adventures with a unicorn family? If so, these experiences will be molding the myth, which becomes the primary bonding instrument in a close-knit group.

You almost had to have been there to fathom how daffodils, or pterodactyls, or space ships could matter so much to a bunch of three-year-olds. While it is an insider phenomenon, the myth is by no means exclusive. Sharing the myth can be a gesture of giving, as when you include the children's parents, or bring a new child into the group.

The group myth transcends any curriculum or planning. Without following a time-table or a prescribed path, the myth just happens, enriching the fabric of your home child care experience. You'll only "find" group myth by being open to it. I try to let go of myths belonging to past groups and embrace each new myth as it unfolds.

You won't reach this masterful level of caregiving all the time. Some days, combinations of children and families, and your own personal problems interfere with your ideas. Children arrive late and grumpy, parents forget their child's swimsuit and you didn't get to the library as you had planned. On days like that, it's a real joy to enlarge on a spontaneous idea from one of your children.

Sometimes an activity, a focus outside themselves and their problems, can nudge the children back toward delight and joy in life. I say "toward" because there's never any guarantee that your children will be happy, your days run smoothly, and your work ring with

I've learned I can't make "the magic." I can, though, through attentiveness to our special group, and planning, help it along.

satisfaction. When it all comes together and everything works, you feel like an angel among shining stars. I call those times "the magic." Usually individual interests or aspects of the group myth usher in those magical moments. I've learned I can't *make* "the magic." I can, though, through attentiveness to our special group, and planning, help it along. When the magic does come, I just enjoy!

Organic learning, like group myth and magic, is something we often bump into, rather than plan. The way one of my day care groups hit upon making journey cakes is a good example. One day, as I was reading the old tale *JOURNEY CAKE, HO!* by Ruth Sawyer, we began to wonder what a journey cake tastes like. "We should make one sometime," I unthinkingly proposed. "When?" my five-year-old demanded. Knowing me pretty well, he thought it best to pin me down. "Tomorrow?" he pressed. Well, I hadn't planned to make journey cakes the very next day..., but as I thought about it, why not? It would fit in with an experimenting project we had just begun. (See Chapter 5 for more on "Experimenting.") In this case, we could experiment with how to make a journey cake. The children had made lots of muffins from scratch, so they knew the basic ingredients. We would just have to make the journey cake so that it could cook in a fry pan, like the old woman's. As I generally look for opportunities to show the children we needn't be deterred by limitations (such as no recipe) I had the feeling there was no turning back. I turned the idea around in my head as the children waited. It would be a fun project, but it would also be hard to keep order because the little

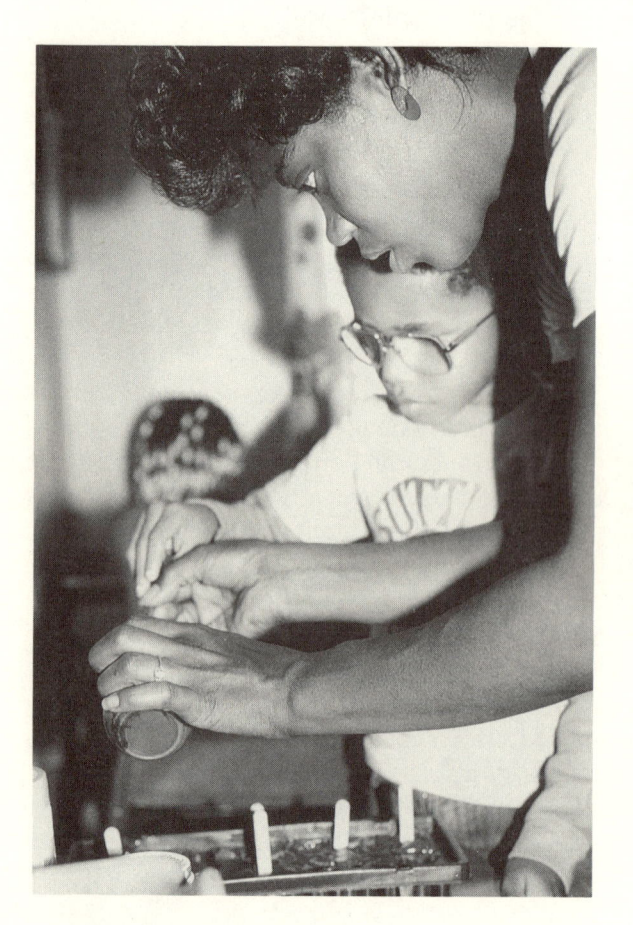

By paying attention to special interests and planning ahead, you can make special moments happen.

Expanding Your Program 57

ones insist on being included. But my nervousness about seven children with vinegar and soda experiments the day before had been unfounded. That activity had gone just fine! So, bracing myself for whatever unexpected mess lay ahead, I agreed that, tomorrow, we would make journey cakes, ho! And they were delicious!

More Activities To Fall Back On

Developing activities that come right out of your own experience of living with children often results in the very best projects and those memorable times when the children are most involved. Be sure to put this book aside when everything's really flowing. Trust yourself and the children. Then bring it out again for the low ebb days when it's difficult to get that spark or you're feeling overwhelmed. Some of my fiascos and absolute treasures may remind you of your own. I hope my experiences will encourage you to find new ways to put organic pzaz into the lives of your children. Until then, try...

Projects

Foot Painting

Foot painting isn't as daring as it sounds. Yet it's so appealing it's always the picture in the photograph album that new children pull me back to and remind me that I promised them this activity. Squishing in paint seems adventuresome and even, almost, naughty. Every child should get to paint with his/her feet, at least once a year.

On a Mural

Stretch a long sheet of butcher paper across your kitchen or playroom floor. Have the children tape it down. Get two rubber dishpans. Mix tempura paints with a little water in one and leave that dishpan on the counter temporarily. Mix soap and warm water in the other. Place the soapy water, a stack of towels and a low chair, at the far end of the paper. While you're preparing, the children can be taking off their shoes and socks. You may need to help roll up their pantlegs. I put a playpen next to the painting for all the little ones under two. A high chair would do. Any bruised egos can be salved by proclaiming that these are the grandstand seats. Then I draw an imaginary line along the floor about a foot from the paper. The children stand along this line. For particularly excitable children, we move in a row of child-sized chairs; some get to be the audience while they wait for their turns to paint.

Usually, I go first. No one can believe I'd put my feet in that green paint! But I do, and they giggle and carry on.

Usually, I go first. No one can believe I'd put my feet in that green paint! But I do, and they giggle and carry on. I walk, crooked toe and all, to the end of the paper, making lovely big prints. My going first makes the expectations clear. They watch me sitting on the chair, washing my feet in the dishpan and wiping them dry before I join the audience.

Then I escort the first child through the process. Paint can be slippery, so I hold the painter's hand. For more involvement, a second child can hold the other hand, or the older ones hold the youngers. I've never lost a set of clothes to this activity, but it could happen. The youngest watch, wide-eyed, but when it's their turn, they're not about to put their feet in green paint! A hand print or even one finger print will make them part of the group painting.

When we're finished, we have a beautiful, big mural. The first print of each person is labeled, and the project promptly hung. Parents and unsuspecting visitors find it quite a conversation piece.

On individual papers

Cut the paper into large circles or triangles. Then let each child foot print or actually foot paint on their own paper. I did this outside one year. It would have been a successful project if the wind hadn't come up. The first children's painting, lovely and colorful, kept blowing off the clotheslines and sailing across the yard, invariably into the next painter. That would've been a day to catch us on video!

More variations

Sidewalk or patio foot painting would allow more freedom. And you could hose away the paint whenever you wanted, so paint wouldn't be tracked in the house. I'd like to see the children get a chance to foot paint up and over a cardboard house. I haven't tried this one, but I know they'd love it.

Foot painting is activity some children will love; others will resist.

Expanding Your Program

Just be sure to set limits and be clear about what's okay with you and what's not!

Cornmeal and Water

This is one activity that can be best summed up by: I don't know what possessed me!

Well, I do know, actually. I wonder if you've had days like this? All the children were seated at the card table. I was getting out mixing bowl, measuring cups, and playdough ingredients. I hadn't planned playdough for that day; we needed something to pull us out of a bickering morning. As I was collecting the ingredients, I realized, much too late, that I was out of both oil and salt. How could I have been so short-sighted? And what could I do with six children, all finally sitting cooperatively at a very small table?

I discarded several possibilities: Cornmeal play? No, spilling from a high table would get it all over the floor, and, by the time I would have cleaned up, we'd have it all over the house, too. Painting? No, there wasn't enough room, and I wasn't about to choose which children had to leave the table to wait. Coloring? No, not captivating enough for that morning's energy. After all, they did deserve a reward for deciding to be pleasant with each other.

Cornmeal, cornmeal, cornmeal, what could I do with cornmeal? Before I really thought about the consequences, I was putting aside the playdough ingredients and pulling big pans out of the stove drawers. Then I got out dishpans from under the sink and stainless steel bowls off the shelf—enough large containers for everyone.

"We don't have the ingredients for playdough, "I heard myself say, "but we do have cornmeal for an experiment." As their eyes got bigger, I poured a mound of cornmeal in each container. "Wait just a minute, now." (I didn't want that dry cornmeal everywhere.) I followed right after with a pitcher of warm water, and, hard as it is to believe now, I told them, "Okay, you may go ahead and mix it." "With our hands?" they asked; "Yes," I answered, and before I got out any cautioning instructions, all hands were gooey. We poured in more water, and they watched pools form in the pockets of coagulated cornmeal. I found cups and spoons enough to share. They poked holes, filled cups and squished with their fingers some more. My memory blanks a little at that point. I suppose it wasn't long before the fun wore out. I do remember that somebody had the idea to plaster a forearm, then another, then splat, splat on their wrists and

As I was collecting the ingredients, I realized, much too late, that I was out of both oil and salt. How could I have been so short-sighted?

palms, Splat! splat! on an elbow. I stood by aghast.

What bothered me most was that I had done this to myself! The children were doing as I had instructed and were having a ball, and I was getting deeper and deeper in trouble. The more fun they had and the more creative they got, "Experimenting," the more I tried to pull strength from the counter I leaned on. Then, I remember, the phone rang. I had to answer and get right off, as the children had begun their exodus to the sink.

Cornmeal doesn't rinse easily. Shirts were splattered, so most needed a change. Cleanup was chaos, and I'd made a real mess. But, in an exhausting sort of way, I felt satisfied that we had pushed our limits of acceptable fun. I dozed in my chair during naptime, rather than writing my usual notes home. The children had lots to tell their families that evening. (I don't think the parents ever heard from me about it.) The point is, all manner of child caregiving days *will* occur.

Cornmeal in Wading Pool

Another morning during that long winter, I started brainstorming again. This time when I came up with cornmeal, I managed to control myself and leave out the water.

I brought the summer wading pool up from the basement before everyone arrived. With the children seated on the floor around it, I filled the bottom of the pool with cornmeal. They played for the longest time, using matchbox cars and sharing a construction set, and only a little spilled on the floor.

Rubber Band Pictures

A twelve-inch-square piece of plywood for each child can make the base for a fine wall hanging. The children hammer small nails into whatever pattern or non-pattern they choose. (You might have to tap in the nails a little for the younger children.) Then they stretch colored rubber bands between the nails to make the finished picture, one they can change as they move the rubber bands.

Clay

Now and then I like to offer clay as another sculpting media, even though clay carries images of figurines and pottery. It's an easy medium to store, as a well-wrapped block of clay can last you a couple of years. Remember that the finished product isn't important; it is the process of working with a new material that counts. Because

---

The children were doing as I had instructed and were having a ball, and I was getting deeper and deeper in trouble.

of its density, simple rolling, cutting, or building with clay can tax preschoolers. Often all they want to do is pull off little bits to stack on other little bits. I've sent home the most nondescript assortment of clay treasures at times. No matter; whatever their level of involvement, the children always want to do more.

Colored-Yarn Sculpture

I know you're going to say, "There she goes again." But, really, this idea was an inspiration. You'll need to have an assortment of small boxes and short strands of thick yarn ready ahead of time.

First, I passed out the boxes. While the children taped or glued them together, snipping and folding as they needed, I mixed up some flour and water, dividing the goop into a number of small bowls. Then I let the children tint the mixture with different combinations of food coloring. One strand at a time, they dipped the yarn into a bowl, then draped, twisted, and piled the yarn onto their sculptures. Some of the constructions fell over and some had no shape whatsoever, beyond a gooey blob. The sculptures wouldn't have won any prizes, but the fun of making them just might have!

Remember that the finished product isn't important; it is the process of working with a new material that counts.

Clean Up

Here's another good rainy day activity. Like sand or cornmeal, water is very soothing. Make sure each child has a change of clothes first, and crank up the heat. Then place large towels on the kitchen floor, one in front of each child. Next, put a basin of warm water beside each child. If you have them, give everyone a small sponge. Then pass out all the plastic toys you can find. The activity? Letting the children give a good spring cleaning to their playthings. By the time they're through, each child has a towel full of clean and drying toys. Of course, everyone is thoroughly wet and needing a change, but the time has been happily and productively spent. The children are calm, the toys are clean, and so is the floor!

Watch out for the toddlers: the floor may be slippery as you're picking up basins and getting everyone dried off.

A Not-So-Wet Variation

We make cleaning the chairs and table an activity, too. First the children line all the chairs in a row. (Thankfully, we have an oak set with very good seal.) Using warm, wet cloths, each child takes a chair, and the big children tackle two. Even the one-year-olds do the best they can to wipe down rungs, back, and seat. Then everybody washes the table together. While the furniture dries, we all pile on the couch for stories. At lunchtime, the children beam over their work.

Concept Games

Every one of us has moments when we can't muster inspiration. Suppose you finish an activity early. You've picked up the toys, and there are still twenty minutes before the kindergartners arrive for lunch. You know the little ones won't want that stopgap stack of puzzles again. Or the "What-will-I-do-now?" scenario strikes you at the end of the day when everyone's tired and the length of the wait may be unpredictable, depending on the parents. You clamp down on the impulse to holler, "Can't you just be quiet and wait for your parents to come?" To prevent such outbursts, I began a repertoire of games that required my involvement with the children.

Besides the traditional and well-loved "Ring Around The Rosey," "Motor Boat," "London Bridges," and "Red-Light Green-Light," lots of games for older children can be adapted for this age. *The New Games Book* by New Games Foundation is full of non-competitive games. Since there is such a wealth of preschool game ideas available, I'd like to focus here on some play-acting concept games, ones that nurture ideas you're trying to impart. You can invent your own, as each new group (adults included) will have their own particular needs and feelings to work on.

Stop And Think

A few years ago I had a group with one boy that was substantially older than the rest. He would come up with unacceptable and sometimes unsafe things for the younger ones to do.

A few years ago I had a group with one boy that was substantially older than the rest. He would come up with unacceptable and sometimes unsafe things for the younger ones to do. This originated more from his active imagination and impish streak than it did from any maliciousness. I talked privately with the parents and with the boy himself. But, as the problem wasn't going to right itself overnight, I needed the other children to be able to say "no."

That's how "Stop and Think" began. I'd lead everyone in a "Do this, then this," until we got to an unreasonable direction. "Go up on the porch. Hop up and down. Climb up onto the railing and jump off." Whenever the children felt cautious, they'd yell "Stop and think!" Then everyone had to sit down as fast as they could. Once out of danger, they'd discuss whether this was really an okay command to follow, or whether they should say, "No!" In order to decide, I encouraged them to say it in an "if" sentence. (e.g., "If I jump off the porch,...I might get hurt.") An acceptable alternative would be chosen, one everyone could act out together. Getting their whole bodies involved carried the lesson a step beyond lecture. It also gave the oldest child a real chance to take a turn leading in a positive way.

This dramatic play can be extended to taking candy from strangers, thinking out what to do in emergencies, etc. One parent who teaches at the middle school told me that if this practice could be ingrained at an early age, so much agony would be saved later on, when peer pressure reaches its peak.

Watch The Donut, Not The Hole

Another concept game came out of "the whiner syndrome." Some children (some adults for that matter) always look at the negative side of things. They notice that I only treated them to a mini ice cream cone rather than a giant size; whereas other children might be glad of a cone at all. Or, children who whine, bemoan the fact that we have three good trikes at the moment, rather than devising a system to share the three until the fourth is fixed.

This attitude towards life, of fussing and focusing on what's lacking rather than rejoicing in what's present, is as infectious as the flu. Even the cheeriest caregiver can be discouraged by a child who constantly whines. You need an immediate way to counteract the behavior before it spreads.

I try to play this game at pleasant times, not when I'm feeling irritated by the child who is being negative. That way, the child has a chance to jump in on the positive, rather than to be defensive.

I try to play this game at pleasant times, not when I'm feeling irritated by the child who is being negative. That way, the child has a chance to jump in on the positive, rather than to be defensive. I'm grateful for the Burl Ives song "Watch the Donut, Not the Hole" as the inspiration for this play. The concept is a tough one for preschoolers. But by play-acting, picking out a half-eaten or half-remaining watermelon, a windy yet sunny day, a bumpety yet serviceable wagon, even two-year-olds catch on. Again, getting the children's whole bodies involved, either by pretending to "be" things or by scurrying around trying to find different items, helps them internalize the concept. After a few sessions of "Watching the Donut, Not the Hole" playing, I've heard a child chide another, "We don't have chocolate chips, but we *do* have cookies!"

Building on the positive when everyone is feeling good is relatively easy and it carries over to help when children are feeling negative.

Most parents and caregivers try very hard to relate fairly and equally to their children. The children benefit from our calm assertion, "It works out in the long run." They don't enjoy the fierce competition any more than we enjoy getting pulled into it.

Long Run/Short Run

I've tried to work on "The Long Run/Short Run" concept, but with little success. Siblings, or children in day care who become very much like siblings after several months together, tend to push for absolute fairness. "He got more than I did!" Whether it's juice in a glass or a turn being listened to, the extent to which this gets carried can try anyone's patience. So we explore "In the long run it works out even; in the short run it may not." That means I don't *have* to get all the portions equal, or I don't *have* to watch exactly two minutes of each puppet show. Most parents and caregivers try very hard to relate fairly and equally to their children. The children benefit from our calm assertion, "It works out in the long run." They don't enjoy the fierce competition any more than we enjoy getting pulled into it.

If this concept comes across as "lecturey," you're right. I haven't moved it very well into the play-acting realm. Perhaps some of you will devise a way to incorporate it into play.

Bouncing Game

One last concept game gives you an example of changing negative behavior into positive interactions simply by turning it into a game. I stumbled onto this idea the day before spring vacation, when my "bouncingest" child started bouncing on the couch. Instead of humiliating her with "Don't!" I made her feel as if she'd invented something. "What a great springy idea!" I said, as I led her by the hand to the floor. I started to bounce, too. We bounced "over a mountain," "into the washing machine," and "onto an elephant." The children suggested more places. We bounced and bounced all over the house until we all got the giggles and fell in a heap. It was better than making my bouncing "tigger" sit in a chair, because she needed to bounce. None of us will always hit on the most delightful response to the children. Be glad and give yourself credit when you do. If you keep a mental list of behaviors that need attention, you are more likely to do purposeful activities during those in-between waiting times.

Games To Stimulate The Intellect

Thinking games, such as these, will also help smooth the rough spots in your day:

Print Identification

First, assemble a collection of print-makers like forks, popsicle sticks, donut cutters, pieces of string, balls, and plastic cups. Pass out the playdough to the children, then have them pat it out flat. Tell them to close their eyes and make a print on each piece of playdough. With their eyes open, have the children identify the printer.

You can increase the challenge by making prints with objects of similar shape. See if the children can guess what made the print just by feeling it, without opening their eyes.

Sequence Exercises

Lead the children in a simple clapping rhythm, and have them imitate the sequence. You can make it more difficult with each round. Vary this game by leading with pats on your head, shoulders, tummy, etc. while the children follow. Let each of them lead a sequence, one at a time.

Sequence Cards

Draw pictures on small cards showing the sequence of a growing flower: the bare ground, a seed planted, a sprout, a stem and two leaves, a bud on the stem, an open bloom, and a wilted flower on the ground. You will need to go through the sequence once, then shuffle the cards and ask the children to arrange them in order.

Make up cards with other sequences, such as a child growing from a baby into an adult, or a child moving through a typical day care day. Stick-figure drawings are fine.

One child told me, "First there's a good light bulb. Then you turn the switch on and off, on and off. And finally it burns out."

Have the children help you think up more sequences. One child told me, "First there's a good light bulb. Then you turn the switch on and off, on and off. And finally it burns out." Some sequences may be harder than others to illustrate.

Classifying Objects

Cut out six or so magazine pictures of a certain category of item: animals, furniture, plants, or people. Ask the children to sort the pictures into groups, putting like things together. You can make this a more difficult task by asking the children to arrange a set that has one each of the different categories. Some children may do further sorting, such as people according to eye color or furniture according to use.

Twenty Questions

Classifying objects will prepare the children for "Twenty Questions." The person who's "it" says, "I'm thinking of something...." When asked questions, he/she answers only "yes" or "no". Younger children, of course, will spill the beans at times, giving eager and obvious hints. In a very short while, though, the children will begin interjecting abstracts such as "the universe," "happiness," or "nothing!"

Concentration

Most of you are familiar with the parlor game "Concentration." A tray is filled with miscellaneous items, and each item is identified for the group. The person who's "it" gets to look at the tray for a limited time, and then she leaves the room. Each remaining person removes an item from the tray. Upon her return, "it" tries to recall the missing items.

I've been surprised at how much the children like this game. They may have seen older family members play it and they feel happy that they're old enough to play such a hard game. Even young two-year-olds enjoy being "it," although they have a difficult time keeping their items concealed while others are guessing. Three and four-year-olds play Concentration very well and they would play it every day if I let them. I try to save it for the days when I'm desperate for a fill-in game because it only takes a second to grab a tray and scrounge a handful of unusual items from the "junk drawer" to play Concentration.

Sensory Awareness Games

You can surprise them by interspersing the voice from someone in their families in among the other sounds on the tape.

Sound Games

Using a portable tape recorder, lead the children around your home as you record sounds. You might record the sounds of magic markers squeaking on paper, water dripping into a pan, or wooden blocks clacking together, etc. Then gather the children around you and replay what you've recorded. Pause after each sound, so they can identify what they hear.

Later, record familiar sounds yourself, without the children's help, and see if they can identify the sounds. You can surprise them by interspersing the voice from someone in their families in among the other sounds on the tape.

Hidden Noise

Hide a wind-up toy or transistor radio in a drawer, cupboard, or closet, and the children take turns finding it. Then let them hide it from you. If your family owns several radios, hide more than one, all set at the same station. My son tricked me once, not with one or two radios, but with five radios all blaring away.

Sniffing Jars

Wrap a number of baby food jars in construction paper. Fill each with a different substance: dirt, vanilla, cinnamon, tomatoes, rose petals, toothpaste, nutmeg, etc. Ask the children to close their eyes and, one by one, to smell and identify the contents.

What's in the Bag?

You've probably played this game's scary version at a teenage Halloween party, with bags of peeled grapes, cooked spaghetti, etc. A tamer, straightforward guessing game version offers as much fun and challenge for preschoolers. After you've played "What's in the Bag?" with miscellaneous items, try a more difficult round using items that are similar, such as a rubber ball, golf ball, and tennis ball, pieces of string, yarn, and twine, cubes, spheres, and pyramids, etc. You can put everything back in the bag and give directions for each turn, too: "Take out a soft item... Now take out something hard... Take out the longest piece of string," etc.

What's in the Bag? can be played out of different sized bags, from a paper lunch bag to a pillowcase. The larger the bag, the sillier the game, as the children have to reach way into the bag. Be sure to stay away from plastic bags of any sort because of the danger of suffocation. Caution the children, if they play the game at home, to use only paper bags and remind them why.

How Does It Feel

Textures can be learned through games. The children can examine and put into order swatches of material or pieces of sandpaper from roughest to smoothest. Walk around the house looking for five smooth and five rough surfaces. You can think up other textures for the children to locate: bumpy, curvy, straight, etc.

As you look for other ways to turn learning into short little games, don't overdo the "teaching." There's nothing worse for a child than to have an adult turn every experience into a lesson. Your presence and honest interest is more valuable than lessons. We need to let children be children, playing and exploring on their own. We can add to their awareness and ability to function in the world by exploring with them, and offering them fun ways of learning through short games.

We need to let children be children, playing and exploring on their own. We can add to their awareness and ability to function in the world by exploring with them, and offering them fun ways of learning through short games.

Chapter 5
Rounding Out Your Program

As you consider how to take activities and interests yet one more step, you'll find yourself an increasingly challenged and satisfied caregiver.

Now that you have a basic program underway, you can begin to look at enrichment opportunities. The following sections outline some possible options you might consider. Activities like cooking and creative movement can be fit into your regular program, perhaps on a weekly basis. For others, like gardening and experiments, you may want to schedule a block of time over several days to allow for a complete unit study. Or, you may expand on some of your units every three months or so by following animal or plant study through seasonal cycles.

All these activities add richness and depth to your caregiving. As you consider how to take activities and interests yet one more step, you'll find yourself an increasingly challenged and satisfied caregiver.

Cooking

Cooking is one of my least favorite activities, but I do a fair amount of it with the children because it's so good for them. Measuring, mixing, kneading, pouring, washing, and chopping help those little fingers become more coordinated and give children real life practice in math. Children feel so good about themselves after they've made a batch of muffins or homemade soup, and they always eat better if they've made it themselves. If you have any doubts, let your three-year-old assemble a salad. He'll be dishing it up for everybody, with several bowls for himself. I'm always surprised by parents who won't let their children help in the kitchen until they're ten or twelve. Children can be very capable cooks, even at two and three.

Before I begin a cooking year, I establish ground rules. I let the children know this is not *the* way to cook; it is simply one way, the way that works best for me with groups of children. I alter recipes freely to make the process simpler, such as mixing the dry things in one bowl, the wet in another, then adding all at once.

Many parents encourage nibbling and tasting as you go, but I don't. I've gone through too many winters of constant colds and runny noses to want to serve, let alone eat, anything made with all those little fingers in the bowl. For cooking in a group, we always wash hands first, then we use spoons and measuring cups. There maybe is just a little finger-licking after all is done and in the oven. What families allow at home needn't contradict your methods, or vice versa, as long as the expectations are clear to the children.

Most children enjoy cooking. By setting ground rules and adapting recipes to children's abilities, you can have successful cooking experiences.

Muffins

A simple muffin recipe works well for beginning cooks because it teaches the concepts of wet and dry. We put all the wet ingredients in one bowl, the dry in another, then we mix the two types together.

1 cup white flour	3 Tbsp. honey
1 cup whole wheat flour	1 well-beaten egg
2-1/4 tsp. baking powder	3/4 cup milk
3/4 tsp. salt	1/3 cup melted margarine

Bake in greased muffin tins 2/3 full at 400° for 25 minutes. Medium sized muffin tins are nice for snacks. Then the older children can have two, without getting so full they won't eat their lunches.

For variety we invent our own muffins. Using the basic recipe, we add any of the following:

raisins
blueberries
grated cheese
sauteed onion and our home-grown herbs
jelly
or ???

Ice Cube Jello

Help the children mix up a batch of jello, using only half the water required, and put it into small pitchers. Let each child fill two or three sections of a molded ice cube tray. Refrigerate as usual.

When it is solid, slip a knife in at each edge to pop out the jello cubes. The cubes will be hard enough to eat with your fingers.

For variety, the children can slip a banana slice into each section before the jello sets. Or you can make layered jello by waiting a half hour between batches, then pouring a second flavor over the first.

This recipe can also be made without sugar by using gelatin with unsweetened pineapple juice, heated as you would the water.

Cookie Cutter Sandwiches

Children can make their own special sandwiches by cutting bread into cookie cutter shapes. Open-faced sandwiches work well; the pieces don't have to match. And the bread trimmings come in handy if you feed ducks or pigeons at a park.

The children will create new sandwiches and your only problem may be finding a platter big enough.

Sandwich possibilities: Spread the bread with margarine, then spread on softened cream cheese or peanut butter and jelly. Or allow the children to put on slices of bologna, pepperoni, banana, or cucumber. The children will create new sandwiches and your only problem may be finding a platter big enough.

Fresh Orange Fruit Cups

Gather the children in a circle and play catch with as many oranges as you have children. The children needn't be concerned if they drop one, because a little bumping about is a prerequisite to squeezing the oranges.

Next, have everyone wash their hands and an orange. Cut each orange in half. Let the children take turns squeezing the oranges in a hand-held juicer.

Pour the juice over the contents of a can of fruit cocktail. Freeze the mixture in a pan just until slushy, then dish it into fruit cups and eat!

For variety add lime or grapefruit juice, or top with fresh orange slices.

Baby Pizzas

The children can help you mix the dough.

To:
    1 pkg. yeast, dissolved in
    1/2 cup of lukewarm water
    with a drizzle of honey

Add:
    1-3/4 cups flour
    1/2 tsp. salt
    1/4 cup salad oil

After the dough is thoroughly mixed, pass out small portions so that each boy and girl can knead his/her own. Then have the children press their dough into a small circle, flattening it into a greased baking dish. Each child can spread on his/her own tomato paste. Place a sprinkle of dried oregano or basil in each of their hands, so they can crumple it onto their pizzas. Then let them choose their toppings from:

olives
finely chopped celery
pepperoni, ham, or other meat
small pieces of pineapple
grated cheese

Bake at 400° for 15 minutes. Enjoy!

Sprouts

With increased nutrition awareness these days, we day care providers look for any opportunity to offer vegetables and other healthy snacks. Children can cultivate a taste for sprouts, especially when they've been involved in growing them. This is a good ongoing project that you can repeat once a week. Sprouts that don't get eaten can be fed to an appropriate pet.

Use: Alfalfa seeds   Mung beans
       Lentils   Other sproutable legumes

Day 1: Before the children leave for home, have them pour seeds in separate jars, filling each about one quarter full. Then pour in water, nearly to the top of the jars.

Day 2: First thing in the morning have the children pour off the water. I use either a small strainer or wire mesh attached to the top of the jars with rubber bands. Place the jars in a dark cupboard for the first day. (Combine Day 1 and Day 2 for alfalfa seeds; they don't require long soaking.)

Day 3: Pour water over the sprouts again, then drain off immediately. Place the jars in the light.

Repeat Day 3 procedure each day until the seeds sprout. Sprouting will take from two to five days, depending on the type of seeds.

Eat the sprouts plain or serve with chopped cucumbers, radishes, carrots, and tomatoes, which the children chop themselves. You may want to toss with a light Italian dressing.

Quesedillas
You'll need:
- corn or flour tortillas
- cheese
- vegetable oil

Have the older children grate cheddar or mozzarella cheese. We like a little of both. Next, have each child sprinkle some cheese on a tortilla and put another tortilla on top. One at a time, place the tortillas carefully in a fry pan with the bottom covered in hot oil. This and any step involving a burner, particularly with hot oil, should be done by the adult. Heat until lightly browned, but not crunchy, then turn. Heat the second side and serve on plates.

You might want to cut the quesedillas in half or in small wedges, depending on the children's appetites. Even with this minimal involvement, the children feel like they've "made" their snacks. Quesedillas are good for variety, good tasting, and, again, very healthy.

Variations: Have the children chop tomatoes, mild green peppers, lettuce, and olives. If, after the tortillas are cooked, you open the quesedillas and let the children add their own special touches, they'll eat these vegetable quesedillas and they'll probably ask for more.

Vegetable Soup
With supervised cutting, this can be a very satisfactory project. Have the following ingredients ready:

stock or soup broth concentrate

an assortment of vegetables such as:

carrots	corn
zucchini	celery
potatoes	string beans

Usually they don't even bother picking out the vegetables they "don't like," especially if I've remembered to comment on how different and good everything tastes in THEIR soup.

It's not necessary to sauté the vegetables first, although they are a little tastier that way. Usually I just get a big pot of broth or water boiling. Starting with the longest cooking vegetables, the children chop them, and I put the cut pieces into the pot. Add your own choice of seasonings: thyme, garlic, salt, marjoram, etc. The children can sprinkle what you need into a dry bowl, and then you pour the seasonings into the pot. Alphabet, wagon wheels, or other interesting macaroni can be added for the last twelve minutes.

When the children have helped cook the soup, they all eat big bowls of it. Usually they don't even bother picking out the vegetables they "don't like," especially if I've remembered to comment on how different and good everything tastes in THEIR soup.

Don't be afraid to try your own recipes. At worst you come out with minimal involvement, maximum mess, or simply one of those culinary flops. At best you create a new taste treat that the children will enjoy for years.

Check your local library for more cooking with children recipes.

Gardening

Gardening is a good way to teach a real-life skill to children. It is a skill they can enjoy their entire life.

Gardening should be reserved for the hardy child caregiver, as it embraces two conflicting interests. A friend of mine once said, "You can't grow flowers and kids both." Since she had three trampling boys, I thought she should know. To plant, prune, water and otherwise nurture growing things, care must be taken. Two-year-olds can, and do, obliterate a garden as fast as any natural blight. But over the years, I've come to disagree with my friend. Something about gardening attracts little ones, something more than the dirt. Children can be encouraged while they're with you ("We don't strip the tree bark here; that's like its skin.") to develop the sensitivities required in gardening. And, in my list of priorities, the effort's well worth making. Some children have a greater affinity to growing things than others. They stay longer when we're planting, and care more deeply. But all children jump and holler "I want to" whenever I announce that we're gardening that day.

Before getting the children started, you will need to mentally go through the "what-ifs." For instance, with two children shoveling or hoeing is possible. With six it is not. Shovel handles or rake tongs are dangerous among that many little ones. So, as when we planted nasturtiums, have your garden spot prepared ahead of time.

Things children can do:

- Pick out rocks.
- Put in worms gathered from under rocks or other areas of the yard.
- Place stones around the garden, so little ones won't step where flowers are planted.
- Put up name stakes, if necessary.
- Plant seeds or seedlings.
- Water with a small watering can, so the seeds won't be washed away.

I try to make sure that the planting space has adequate room around or in front so that everyone can stand and watch at once. Otherwise, while one child is bending over to plant, a back-row waiter may push or be pushed, and the next thing you know you've planted a child, head first. Planting seeds is so simple, especially ones that are the size of peas. It helps if your seeds are large enough for children to grasp easily. All the children need to do is poke and pat. Be sure to choose seeds that aren't chemically treated.

After "poke and pat," I fill the watering can so each child can have a turn. We talk quite naturally, as we stand around the garden, talking about what makes a seed grow. More than once the sun has magically appeared from behind the clouds at this moment. We all giggle and exclaim, "Hooray for the sun!" Before the children disperse, we sing "Happy Growing To You" (Happy Birthday tune). Then the children scatter to trikes, slide, or hiding places.

But they all return to look and poke and wonder when the seeds will be up. I like the absence of fences around the borders; I like the children to feel there's an open door to their garden. As long as a few of the older ones will stay outside, they help the little ones remember to stay out of the garden. We all get to watch as the first sprouts come up out of the dirt and spread first two leaves, then four, and spread some more. Pretty soon the children are dancing about, with shouts of "Look, they're growing!" Eventually, even the least interested child stops to gaze in wonder at the bright blooms.

I love flowers more than clothes and furniture. I love to help children love them, too. It does pain me to see a young child pick a lone and rare variety of daffodil, but I believe that a bud or blossom accidentally sacrificed is well worth the child's delight and involvement. Gardening touches the children's souls. My little one used to

It does pain me to see a young child pick a lone and rare variety of daffodil, but I believe that a bud or blossom accidentally sacrificed is well worth the child's delight and involvement.

open tulips with "I peeky boo, Mommy," or push the black centers of the anemone; "Tummy button!" she'd squeal. But she did so lovingly, and, probably because of her early interest, will always be a gardener.

With flannelboard stories and little made-up ditties I also teach these gardening lessons:

- We never eat anything outdoors without asking an adult first.

- We don't pick flowers unless an adult has said we can. My phrase has been "Ask the keeper of the garden before you pick the flowers." Nothing so upsets a gardener as to have a passing child denude a favorite bed. I help the children learn this courtesy early in their childhood.

- In the wilds it's also important to pick only a few specimens at a time, leaving lots to reseed for future flowers. In many parks, of course, picking flowers is strictly forbidden. Temperance in flower-picking can be a building block of respect for our larger environment later on.

One planting project surpassed my wildest dreams. I'd bought some crocuses in the fall, and one day I spontaneously decided to ask the children to help me plant them.

One planting project surpassed my wildest dreams. I'd bought some crocuses in the fall, and one day I spontaneously decided to ask the children to help me plant them. Actually, the thought originated with the desperate plight of a transplanted dwarf cherry tree. I had put the tree close to the sandbox, thinking it would be so pleasant to be a child building a sand castle with cherry blossoms overhead. What I hadn't thought out was how inviting the little tree would be for a child that jumped off the sandbox bench and swooped down and around it. The poor little tree was in a definite life-threatening situation. No matter how natural and appealing the swinging around it was for the three to five-year-olds, I had to do something to save it. The idea occurred to me, "If the children help with a rock border and planting, maybe the tree will have a chance to mature."

So our planting was under way. Bulbs are harder to plant than seeds because they must go deeper, but a round stick worked well for boring the holes. Each child carefully placed a bulb at the bottom of their hole and sprinkled loose dirt on top. I squatted next to them, in turn, trying to help them get the "nose" up and the "feet" down. Those bulbs are slippery. But we must have managed to right them all, as they sprouted in the spring in a complete circle. However, every other one did not come out purple, then gold, as I had thought.

I've always contended that children's attention spans and caring are qualities that would astound us if we only believed in and nurtured those capacities. This was a good case in point, as I have never seen a group of children stay with an idea so long.

Instead, they were wonderfully mixed as befitted a children's planting.

But that's getting ahead of the story. For all those months the children remembered the bulbs they'd planted. I've always contended that children's attention spans and caring are qualities that would astound us if we only believed in and nurtured those capacities. This was a good case in point, as I have never seen a group of children stay with an idea so long. And these were one, two, three, and four-year-olds, mind you. Interestingly enough, the five-year-old in our group was the least involved, but that seemed due more to his natural inclination than to his age.

In all sorts of weather the children watched the spot to see how their bulbs were doing. On rainy October mornings, when the moms or dads were struggling to get inside with boot bags and lunch boxes, their absent-minded "Yes, dear" would get them pulled off the path to check on these bulbs. On winter days the children poked into the snow. "Are they still there?" they'd ask. January's sun brought discontent. "But you said they'd come up in the spring!" the children protested. Finally, early in March, there they were.

The first little tips poked through the soil. Then everybody helped me furiously weed out any little grass shoots or chickweed, so the crocuses would have room to breathe. With the littlest children, I

Planting and helping something grow inspires excitement and pride in children.

weeded around the sprouts, and they weeded around the rocks. In just a day or two the leaves grew, and soon a bud was up; in the glorious weather we had as the crocuses sprouted, the blossoms soon followed. And, oh, such happy children! I thought my three-year-old boy's little heart would burst with joy. When he was tired he could be difficult to work with, but give him a flower to plant, watch, and care for, and he turned into an angel personified. His general nature mellowed that year and I often wondered if it had to do with his new-found ability to care for living things. I'm sure I flatter myself, but there's really no way of knowing. Certainly it did him some good.

The first day that we had a profusion of blossoms around the yard, this three-year-old pulled his mom back and forth from one border to the next, saying, "And I want to show you this one...and what is this one called again?"

Some adults are plant-lovers and others are not. I want to challenge you, even if gardening isn't one of your interests, to try just a little planting with your children. We all have a basic need to be connected to our earth and other living things. Perhaps you could invite in a garden club member to lead the lessons if you feel inept. If you don't have a yard, then window boxes, sprout gardens, flower pots, and little seedlings in a cup are all wonderful substitutes.

Herbs make delightful potted gardens. Try an ongoing treat of herb pots by the back door. Thyme, rosemary, and sage all can be used in cooking, and you can have fun guessing the smells. Nurture the children's sensitivities by teaching them to distinguish lemon balm from a row of other crushed herbs. They can do it. Real life activities, like growing mint for tea, prove to be more engaging than playing with toys. Just ask children if they want to pick the herb you need and watch them race for the back door garden.

One year I taught a three, four, and five-year-old class in an upper-middle-class school. The building, then in a rural setting, was being surrounded by a fast developing suburbia. The children there were more familiar with shopping malls than with farms or gardens. However, the school's next door neighbor was a farmer of sorts. I had overheard the neighbor offer to the school's caretaker some horse manure for the flower borders. Since it was thoroughly decomposed manure from several years back, and I knew I could keep the children from playing in it, I leapt at the opportunity to use the manure. I couldn't have taught a better lesson in the cycles of nature

Real life activities, like growing mint for tea, prove to be more engaging than playing with toys. Just ask children if they want to pick the herb you need and watch them race for the back door garden.

than fertilizing our garden with this neighbor's offering.

My ten preschoolers and I trudged on a rooted path, pushing our wheelbarrow through the narrow woods. A made-up planting song, long since lost from memory, helped us hike along. Once we got to the barnyard, there were smirks and giggles, of course. I knew the children had "horse poop" in perspective when they thanked the horse as we left with our full wheelbarrow. And, oh, how our sweet peas were the envy of the whole school!

More recently, as my children watched the crocus wilt and die back, they felt only slight remorse. I've heard them philosophically expound to their parents, who squat by the rocks, listening: "It's okay," the little ones say, "the flowers will go into the dirt. And make it better. And more crocuses will bloom next year."

It's almost time to reseed that spot under the cherry tree. I wonder what we should plant this summer? Pansies or moss roses?

Animal Care

I have two canaries in the kitchen, primarily for my little ones' interest. I'm hoping one day to raise baby canaries. The children help feed the birds, pour water to give them baths, pick dandelions and chickweed for them in the warm months, and cook up carrots for the canaries in the winter. They also enjoy watching me clip the birds' toenails. Only once did our female fly out when a two-year-old opened the cage, but we got her back with no problem.

I often say, "Thank you, Charlie" to the singing male for his song. I hear the children say, "Thank you, Charlie" on their own, especially after he's held a particularly long trill. You can model appreciation in little ways throughout the day, and the children will pick up on these and transfer the caring to family members and friends.

In other caregiving settings I've let the children raise chameleons, hamsters, goldfish, rabbits, turtles, cats, dogs, and even a pet alligator. One year I whelped 12 purebred Standard poodles right in the middle of my home day care. I had the box under the kitchen table. Thankfully, our dog gave enough warning that I had time to warm the babies' bottles, to feed and change them, and to put them down for naps before the birth got under way. Nine puppies were born while the two babies I cared for slept.

What a treat for the next few days! Even though I knew and trusted my dog, I wouldn't have planned to mix child care and a large litter of pups. But now, years later, the kitchen puppies make great

My point is, we all have lives apart from day care that at times merge with our caregiving. As long as you're not letting safety considerations slide, the children benefit when you include them.

Rounding Out Your Program   81

Pets can enrich a child's life so much by encouraging nurturing behavior. But they must be carefully planned for.

memories. My point is, we all have lives apart from day care that at times merge with our caregiving. As long as you're not letting safety considerations slide, the children benefit when you include them. Some of you might raise farm animals in a pasture out back. What a gift you can give your children by allowing them to help care for a newborn.

Children would have us fill our homes with animals. I urge you to first assess what *you* can handle, not necessarily what the children want. Otherwise, you may end up with a menagerie of cranky, perhaps uncared for, and thereby potentially dangerous pets. Nothing bites like a hungry gerbil. One or two pets at a time, though, can be a real delight for everyone. Caring for pets nurtures the ability to care in children.

Our absolute all-time, number-one best pet is in the bathtub at the time of this writing. Several weeks ago I took the children to a Feed and Seed store where we bought a two-week-old duckling. We've watched it grow, feather by feather. And like proud parents, we all feel puffed up with pride over this duck. Although he is almost grown now, he still sleeps in a giant box in the kitchen. He still takes baths in the tub for the fun of it, but he also has his own kiddie pool outdoors. The children have theirs too, and the duck knows the difference. We intend to find him a new home, one with other ducks and a pond. Nobody's quite ready for the parting yet.

A duck that's been well cared for from an egg or baby duckling, won't bite or hiss as some ducks do. In fact, ducks can be quite affectionate. For the first few weeks we had to dry our duckling with a hair dryer after his baths. Ordinarily, oil from the mother duck's feathers rubs onto the duckling, insulating him from wet and cold. Our duck certainly didn't mind the way we did it; he loved the attention, snuggling down in one of the children's laps to be blow-dried.

You'll want to take your neighbors into account in any outdoor pet purchase. If ducks and noise might be a problem, you'll probably want a male, as they "talk" less than females. You'll need to plan for

You will need to take extra time to teach them to handle and care for the pets in order to prevent any harm to the animals.

extra time to clean the duck and the play yard. The returns on this extra effort are worth it. Never would a child know how a wing is formed without getting to watch it day after day. The learning takes place in a relaxed manner, as an integral part of a child's life.

All animal care involves a certain amount of risk. My children once left the chameleon cage outdoors. The sun moved from behind a tree, heating the glass unmercifully. By the time the cage was remembered, the chameleons had died a cruel death. Accidents, mistakes, and pet mortality are ever-present risks. You should be prepared to guide your children through grief if one of your pets dies or becomes lost. You will need to take extra time to teach them to handle and care for the pets in order to prevent any harm to the animals.

Here are a few ways you can maximize your chances for success with pets:

- Talk with your children about what's involved in each pet's handling and care.
- Brainstorm "Do's" and "Don'ts" with the children. They'll be the ones to think up pet play you never dreamed of. Hopefully, you can avoid any mistakes through discussions ahead of time.
- Allow the children to take turns caring for the animal. A weekly chart encourages responsibility.
- Keep a record with the children of the pet's growth, activities, and any changes in appearance.
- Encourage the children to draw pictures and dictate to you their own captions.
- Encourage reading and study about this pet and related ones. What makes one similar or different from another?
- After setting clear guidelines ahead of time, invite the children to bring their pets from home for a pet sharing day, parade, or turn-taking week. You won't want to baby-sit a boa or invite incompatible animals on the same day. Depending on your group size and potential pet population, you might ask the children to bring pictures of their pets instead.

Children can participate in movement activities in a variety of ways. Some will feel more comfortable than others doing these activities and, with patience, all can learn to enjoy them.

Movement

On the other hand, if we are on an imaginary boat trip, I might say, "Now, you lead us when the storm gets really rough." Most children love a chance to direct, and you can always become the leader again any time.

Each of us enriches the children's lives from our own store of abilities and pleasures. Several years ago, in Seattle, I was inspired by Gary Burdge and Len Eisenhood's creative movement classes for children. Since then I've tried to bring that combination of dancing and acting, what teachers call "Movement," to the groups of children I'm with. Even the little ones, who don't start out moving with ease, grow more comfortable as we move together.

If you establish certain ground rules for movement time, you ensure a happy and safe experience. Here are the agreements I set up with the children:

- It's okay to participate by watching.
- We move in our own space. Even if we're all moving around the room, we keep our own spaces, being careful not to bump or kick another person. Sometimes we will intentionally merge our spaces, but only as directed.
- I am the leader for movement, except when I pass the leader's role to a child. This isn't as stifling as it sounds. I can lead the children through a drama, such as a seed sprouting and growing into a tree. Each child expresses this in his/her own way. But, if the children are all talking at once and suggesting different directions, the exploration of that particular drama ends. On the other hand, if we

are on an imaginary boat trip, I might say, "Now, you lead us when the storm gets really rough." Most children love a chance to direct, and you can always become the leader again any time.

- Put-downs are not allowed. Moving, expressing oneself in a group can be scary. We stop whenever we need to, either for the group or for individuals, to talk about feelings. Sometimes it just helps to know others are feeling uncomfortable, too. Or, sometimes, we want to tell everyone how great it felt to move together.

In many movement sessions we use just our bodies. I lead these allowing plenty of time for acting out. I also try to give bits of information to spark the children's imaginations. Instead of just blowing up a balloon, the balloon might have a color, be given to us by a circus clown, but be very hard to blow up. A boat ride might include a description of the boat, such as an outing on an old fishing boat, one that smelled of codfish and clams.

I plan the movement sessions to include one or two exercises from each of the following categories, so the thinking and moving is varied each time.

Instead of just blowing up a balloon, the balloon might have a color, be given to us by a circus clown, but be very hard to blow up.

- **Dramas (Act out...)**

  a balloon blowing up

  a boat ride when a storm comes up

  a seed sprouting and growing into a flower

  a feather floating in the wind and landing on various objects

  a rag doll getting dressed

  an umbrella being caught in the wind and blown open

- **Toys (Pretend you are a...)**

robot	baby carriage
baby doll	block, or together, a set of blocks
rag doll	wind-up monkey
race car	calculator
hula hoop	bouncing ball

- **Animals (all sorts)**

  We sometimes play a very simple game. I sit at one end of the room, and the children line up at the other. One at a time I ask them what kind of animal they are. I might say, "What do you like to eat?" I put pretend bones, grass or whatever they've asked for in a pretend bowl, and they move towards me, "in character," as the animal they are. They eat their food while the next child orders. "Feed the animals" is a simple, silly game, but one the children like very much.

- **Body parts**

  Exercise different body parts, then lead the children in relaxing each part, moving from their heads down to their toes. First lead the relaxation standing up. Then have everyone lie on their backs, and talk them through the relaxation series again, until everyone is as relaxed as possible.

- **Opposites (Act them out)**

heavy and light	thick and thin
big and little	tall and short
giant and tiny	windy and calm

- **Emotions (Act them out using whole bodies, not just faces)**

mad	sad
happy	excited
scared	

Some movement exercises are enhanced by using props.

Some movement exercises are enhanced by using props. Try adding the following to a movement sequence:

scarves	rhythm instruments
balloons	small squares of rug
streamers	balls, large and small
stick horses	

Also, have the children move to different sounds. Tap two sticks together while the children move to the rhythm. Or let them tap paper towel tubes or rhythm sticks, and take turns leading different sequences. Move to bells ringing, a timer ticking, cardboard boxes bumping together, paper rustling, etc. Ask how the children feel in response to the various sounds. Encourage them to listen first, then move. Challenge the children to show the difference in the sounds through their body movements.

Finally, move to records. Your early learning supply store will carry a number of movement choices, but you can lead effective movement and dance to any good rhythm record. Try all sorts of rhythms: jazz, marches, classical, movie soundtracks, popular, rock, country, etc.

Whatever you do with the children, you should practice it and lead yourself through the exercises first. Then you can get the most out of an idea with the children. There's always a fine line when you're actually leading the group: You need to be doing the exercise with them, helping them to explore it to its fullest, but don't be so taken by your own dancing ability that you inhibit the children in theirs.

I schedule certain months of the year with movement classes: twenty minute sessions, two times a week. Maybe I'll continue movement for the first two months of the school year. Then, when Halloween ushers in the holiday season, I might wait until January to lead movement again. These sessions differ from spontaneous movement, which erupts naturally out of the children's play. The stereo might be on, the children's play takes a turn, and suddenly children are dancing. But not everyone dances, and not everyone feels comfortable with movement. In movement class I can gently encourage the children who never dance at all. I can challenge the children who do to explore and express themselves in new ways. The process in movement class helps the children relate to each other with increased comfort and trust, while it nurtures their physical development. As you can see from these few examples, movement sessions are also a lot of fun.

The process in movement class helps the children relate to each other with increased comfort and trust, while it nurtures their physical development.

Experiment

Once, for a group of three to five-year-olds, I wrote the word "Experiment" in large print on the cover of a 15 x 20 inch book. We would do an experiment, then we'd add a new page of pictures and observations to the book. Even non-readers could relate: "You know this word by the X. X marks the spot for something exciting about to happen."

Rounding Out Your Program 87

The activities I list here are ones that can be adapted for many age levels. I got most of them from an elementary science curriculum developed by Leaf Schumann. To engage his classes in the lessons, he'd occasionally dress up in a cape and top hat, wearing a big "D" on his shirt. (Dr. Dynamo is what he called himself.) The children who were fortunate enough to have Leaf for their teacher associated science experimenting with Dr. Dynamo's enthusiasm.

Children are naturally curious experimenters. Having experiments as an activity series gives children the permission to experiment and the parameters to do it safely.

Experiments encourage observation, a valuable skill for all disciplines, not just science. Many comments, sparked by paying attention to the process, accompany each experiment. At this age don't expect scientific deductions. Listen to what the children pick up on, and capitalize on their interests. "Teaching science" isn't important at the preschool level; "doing" is.

Listen to what the children pick up on, and capitalize on their interests. "Teaching science" isn't important at the preschool level; "doing" is.

Be sure to go over experimenting safety. The children need to know that unsupervised experimenting can be very dangerous. Talk about potential household poisons, and familiarize them with poison labels and stickers. Stress that they must always ask an adult before they do an experiment. Inform their parents of the types of activities you'll be doing, so they can go over their safety guidelines at home. Most of these activities and others found in elementary science curriculums are perfectly harmless. We should *NEVER* assume that young children will make knowledgeable decisions, though. They may think, "If it's okay to experiment with kitchen chemicals, then it's probably okay to use these jars from the garage." Firm, clear cautions and "Stop and Think" exercises will give the children the awareness they need to keep from getting hurt. (For more on "Stop and Think" exercises, see Chapter 4.)

The following pages contain experiments suitable for preschool and early elementary school children.

Mixing colors

Materials
- several clear pouring containers
- food coloring

Procedure
- Leaf Schumann would turn this into a magic trick, challenging the children to guess what color would appear next.
- First, fill two jars half full with water.
- Drop food coloring in each jar, red in one, blue in another, or yellow and blue, etc.
- Then pour one jar into the next. (Leaf would chant some hocus-pocus.) "Voila!" a new color appears.
- This can be performed with several jars, several colors, then rinsed and repeated, changing the mixes.
- For more involvement, have easy-to-pour pitchers or baby juice jars, so the children can do the pouring.

Variation on mixing colors

Materials
- ice cube trays, with individual sections
- food coloring
- eye droppers

Procedure
- Fill the ice cube tray 2/3 full with water.
- Drop coloring in several different sections, leaving clear water spaces in between.
- Set up two children at a time, each with an ice cube tray and dropper. The children squeeze color from one section and drop it into another, mixing the colors as they go.

Tip
- The child has to be old enough to squeeze and release the dropper and also old enough to keep the food coloring water from spilling all over him/herself, as food coloring will stain.

Colored lights

Materials
- several colored light bulbs

Procedure
- On a cloudy day when you won't have to compete with bright sunlight, pull the curtains, in either your living room or family room.
- One at a time, put a different color bulb in a central lamp.
- Talk with the children about how the different colors make them feel. Do they have a preference? Do they feel warmer or cooler under a certain light? Does one color make them feel sillier than another? Is another color more soothing?

Tips
- Caution the children to try this experiment at home only with a parent. The children should never be screwing the bulbs in and out.
- Close supervision is essential.

Kitchen chemicals

Materials
- "chemicals" such as
  soda and vinegar
  salt and water
  colored ice and hot water
  ice and cold water
  molasses and soda
  molasses and water
  pepper and water
- other ingredients such as corn starch, sugar, coffee
- stainless steel bowls
- baby food jars
- spoons

Procedure
- Put out sets of chemicals to be mixed in bowls or jars (salt in one jar, water in another, etc.)
- Help establish observation as a part of the experiment. Mix and observe one experiment together.
- Add more sets of chemicals and encourage experimentation.

Tips
- Be careful not to squelch scientific inquiry by conveying preconceived ideas of chemical reactions. Your children may discover something new.
- Go over again that the children are *NEVER* to experiment with any chemicals without asking a parent first.

Variation on vinegar and soda

Materials
- wine bottle and cork
- thin crepe paper streamers
- vinegar and soda

Procedure
- Try this experiment after the children are familiar with the vinegar and soda reaction. However, this experiment is to be performed with an adult.
- First, go outdoors.
- Stick streamers onto top of cork with a straight pin.
- Place 1/4 cup vinegar in bottle.
- Sprinkle in 2 Tbsp. soda.

The children can pour in the vinegar and soda.
- Immediately cork the bottle, being very careful to point it away from people.
- Watch the cork shoot out as the CO_2 is formed.

Tip
- You can write the experiment up as a recipe for the children to do again at home with their families.

Rubber egg

Materials
- jar
- egg, hard-boiled, in shell
- vinegar

Procedure
- Cool the egg.
- Submerge the egg, with the shell still on, in vinegar.
- Wait one week; the shell will completely soften, becoming like rubber.
- This experiment is fun because the children enjoy returning to it every day. "How's our egg doing?" they'll say as they arrive in the morning. Then we get our fingers all vinegary from poking and turning the egg.

Tips
- Make sure the egg is covered in vinegar.
- One year we couldn't remember how to do this experiment, so we tried several eggs, with and without the shell, hard-boiled and raw. Feel free to experiment yourselves.

Sucking the egg into the bottle (the all-time favorite!)

Materials
- an old-fashioned glass milk bottle is perfect, or an empty juice jar with a mouth just smaller than an egg
- match and small piece of paper
- hard boiled egg, peeled

Procedure
- The children sit around a table, giving you plenty of room to carry out the experiment.
- Discuss whether children think an egg can be sucked into a bottle without breaking it.
- Put small piece of paper into the bottle.
- Light the paper.
- As soon as the paper is burning, place the egg on top of the bottle.
- As the fire burns up oxygen, a vacuum is created, which sucks the egg into the bottle.
- Next, discuss how to get the egg out, whole.
- Tilt the bottle up so the egg is resting in the neck.
- Blow into the bottle, getting as much air as possible behind the egg.
- As pressure is created behind the egg, tilt the egg into the opening and it will pop out.

Tips
- The egg will slip in easily if slightly moistened first.

Strong egg

Materials
- clay blob
- raw egg
- plastic sheet, card table, oil cloth, or other protective surface

Procedure
- Place clay on table, on top of protective covering.
- Stick the egg, end up, in clay.
- Try to break the egg by pressing down. The egg won't break if end to end. Have everyone try to break it.
- Place the egg on its side. Press down and watch out!

Magnets

Materials
- magnets, several different sizes
- small metal objects
- an assortment of non-metal objects
- sheet of paper

Procedure
- The children experiment with picking up metal and non-metal objects.

Variation
- Try two people holding a piece of paper, with a metal object on top. Holding the magnet underneath, a third person makes the object move by moving the magnet.

Tips
- This experiment works well in pairs, as you would set up a painting project. The children benefit from working together and from being able to experiment without your help. You can join them towards the end, to take note of their findings.

Check the science section of your local children's library for experiments that can be adapted to your younger age group. Remember, the point isn't to teach scientific concepts but to involve children in positive experimenting. By acknowledging their natural curiosity and by making a big book of their experiments, we nurture self-esteem, and, in yet another way, fill their days with fun, purposeful activity. Experiments could be a once-a-year, month-long focus.

Explore

Exploring, intentional observation, and practice in sensory awareness can be focused into another fun activity series.

Once you've temporarily exhausted experimenting, begin a new book with the children. X can also stand for "Explore." Exploring, intentional observation, and practice in sensory awareness can be focused into another fun activity series.

Begin your exploring in the room you use most. For the first day's activity, simply ask the children to explore that room. Have the children decide how they would like to categorize their observations. If you have a dominant color in the room, ask the children to each draw a picture of one or two things of that color. Together, paste these on a page in your book. Compare the objects, such as toys or furniture, and ask questions about them. How many are made of plastic, wood, or metal? Record these in columns. What kind of heat is there in the room? Lighting? From the children's discussion ideas, determine how much space one child comfortably needs, and have them help establish a maximum comfortable capacity for each room. Record their ideas with diagrams. Draw pictures identifying the sounds you hear. How do the sounds from outdoors affect your indoor environment?

Using the same kind of observation skills, move on to another room. A day or two later, explore the outside. Talk with the children about what is the same and what will be different through the changing seasons. Help them draw pictures to illustrate their observations. Collect leaves for a scrapbook page and record the sounds you hear.

Pick a neighbor in each of the four directions. (Explain your project to the neighbor ahead of time.) Request permission to interview them or to examine their yards. Record your findings. Perhaps one older woman has a doll from her childhood that she will offer to show the children. Or another has a well-stocked fish pool or indoor aviary. You may discover many things you didn't know about your own immediate surroundings.

Encourage the children to explore their own homes, too. Have them bring in sketches of their bedrooms or family rooms. Encourage them to interview their family members, asking questions about their favorite chairs, their favorite spot in the house, the smell they like best. Make a group collage recording their findings.

Finally, have the children pick two favorite pages from your Explore book. Return to these on two separate days. On one day, have the children imagine they're the size of an ant. Use a magnifying glass to reexamine the space. On another day, have them imagine they're giants. Draw pictures to illustrate how the rooms and people in them would look different.

You help the children value their own observations by including your Explore book as a permanent addition to your home library. Let them share it with their parents, or take it with you on trips to the nursing home. There the children can show the pictures and explain about their environment, one on one. Every now and then, on a quiet afternoon, have them take out their book and read through it together.

For exploring further afield, I recommend Rhoda Redleaf's book, *Open the Door, Let's Explore*, a neighborhood field trip guide for young children.

Dramatics

Dramatic activities nurture children's sense of rhythm, sequential thinking, body movement, language development, ability to follow directions, leadership skills, self-expression, and self-esteem.

You've already bought equipment, created the settings, and enjoyed your children's play for hours. Dramatic play simply involves focusing less on the toys and other props and more on the dynamics of pretend. Dramatic activities nurture children's sense of rhythm, sequential thinking, body movement, language development, ability to follow directions, leadership skills, self-expression, and self-esteem. With fairly little effort and no expense, dramatic activities enrich your program and increase your self-confidence right along with the children's. Home day care is a perfect place to begin leading dramatic activities. Since you work alone with children, rather than with your peers, you don't have to be embarrassed when your cat's meow comes out sounding more like a cow's moo.

Fingerplays

Some children, while boisterous in their play, become very inhibited when they're presented with playacting. Finger plays and action songs are a good place to begin because moving hands and fingers are not as threatening as moving one's whole body. Public libraries, book stores, and day care association networks all offer collections of fingerplays. It's a good idea to rehearse even the simplest fingerplay before you try to lead it, so that your rhythm and motion directions are clear.

In addition to the many available published fingerplays, I encourage you to try writing your own. After you've succeeded writing a few yourself, you can involve the children in this creative process. Jot down the lines they come up with, combining and adjusting until you

By writing your own songs and fingerplays, you also get to affirm what has "heart" for your group.

get one with a short, easy rhythm. Once again, since you work alone, the children needn't feel any pressure to make an exceptional song. They derive value simply from trying, from our believing in them, and from their internalizing in yet one more way the "I can" philosophy of life.

By writing your own songs and fingerplays, you also get to affirm what has "heart" for your group. Some of your compositions will speak to your group myth, others will bridge the gap between family and day care, while others will be just plain fun. Here are four that I've written and use with groups of children. My youngest daughter helps me get my ideas into workable form by practicing and editing with me.

"Mama and I"

(or Daddy, Grandma, Sister, etc.)
(Sit in a circle.)

Mama and I	(Put up left pointer then right.)
went out in the sun.	(Make fingers arch over head.)
Mama and I	(Put up left and right again.)
had so much fun.	(Pointers dancing to left and right.)
We swung on the swing.	(One pointer horizontal, the other crossed on top; both swinging.)
We tumbled on the ground.	(Pointers moving around each other.)
We danced with our friends,	(Stand up quickly, holding pointers.)
Round and round.	(Skip around in a circle.)

(Vary the verses with other family members.)

"Feet Move Forward"

(Everyone stand up in a row.)

Feet move forward.	(Walk forward three steps.)
Feet move back.	(Walk backward three steps.)
Feet move side to side.	(Step sideways to the left, then step back to the right.)
Feet move hoppily up and down.	(Jump up and down in place.)
Feet aren't hard to hide.	(Squat down, covering feet with hands and body.)

Repeat with
Hands...
Head...
Whole body...   (Last verse ends, "Whole bodies are hard to hide." Wiggle in a silly way all over, trying to hide yourself.)

"A Unicorn"
(an action rhyme)

A unicorn	
has one horn	(Hold up index finger.)
in the middle	
of her head.	(Point finger out from forehead.)
It's very good	
for pointing the way	(Point from forehead, one way, then the other.)
but not so good	
in bed.	(Lie down, horn first, and bump finger.)
Ow!	
A silly monkey	(Stand up.)
has some funky	(Hold out arms.)
arms that touch	
the ground.	(Bend knees. Stretch arms to the ground.)
They work real well	(Reach up as in swinging.)
for swinging in trees	
but can get twisted	
around.	(Twist arms around self, trip over, fall down.)
Ow!	
A grizzly bear	
has thick hair	(Scratch pretend hair on sides.)
to help him	
through a storm.	(Hug self around shoulders.)
He stays toasty	
in ice and snow,	(Smile, snug and warm.)
but what happens	
when he's warm?	(Hold out collar, panting as if too warm.)
Ah!	
I'm glad I'm me	
with parts, you see,	(Hold up hands, then feet.)
that work	
when I need them to.	
My coat comes off.	(Take off coat.)
I can lie in bed,	(Curl up, as if sleeping.)
and say good-night	
to you.	(Wave good-bye, then tuck head under arm.)

Songs

"Come Run With Me"
by E. Sandy Powell

Come run with me my special friends.
Come sing and dance and play.
Come run with me my special friends.
There's so much to do each day.

I like to make up songs or rhymes that address my pet peeves. A chant or a little tune communicates more gently than repeated lectures. Here are a few instructive songs that I've used. You have your own areas of concern which you can put to rhyme.

"Litter Stamping Chant"

(Stand up. Stamp in place, while moving to words.)

Trash, trash, trash,
I love to smash
it into a little pile.
Shouldn't throw it
or let the wind blow it,
but save it up for awhile.

Pile it, pack it,
Pick it up, stack it.
Recycle whatever you can.
Keep all the rest
in the garbage is best,
for trash, trash, trash, trash, trash.

Discussion: litter; garbage — where it goes; recycling

"Ask the Keeper of the Garden"

Nanny Oldgood grows her roses.
Bampa loves his gladiolas.
Hoeing, seeding, watering, weeding.
Ask the keeper of the garden
Before you pick the posies.

Second verse:
Growing gardens takes long hours.
Work through sunshine, work through showers.
Watching, caring, tending, sharing.
Ask the keeper of the garden
Before you pick the flowers.

From time to time you'll do too good a job. A particular child loves you, loves your activities and your playful attention. When the parent comes at the end of the day, the child won't want to go home. While this is flattering and even amusing at first, it can become a serious problem. The parent may dread the child's daily scene, concerned that you're thinking she/he's a "bad" parent. The child may intensify the drama, wheedling treats and toys in exchange for cooperation. If a peaceful parting can't be achieved on a somewhat regular basis, the parent may even decide to enroll the child elsewhere.

98 Heart to Heart Caregiving

I made up the next tune to offer children an alternative behavior. While the song's not inspired, it does get my point across.

"When My Mom Comes To Get Me"
(or Dad, Grandma, Grandpa, etc.)

When my mom comes to get me
I can make it eas-y.
I won't run and hide my head. I'll pick up all my things instead.
I'll ask, "Can I come back real soon?" I won't make my face like a prune.
If Mommy starts to talk too long, I'll simply sing this little song.
When my mom comes to get me
I can make it eas-y.

If the singsong fingerplays aren't your style, or the children you care for have older siblings who pass on disdain for normal age-appropriate ditties, maybe a "rap" is for you. Try this "Day Care Rap". Experiment and make up your own version. Get out the sandpaper blocks and rhythm sticks, and you've got yourself an activity fit for even the most sophisticated preschoolers.

"Day Care Rap"

Fighting, it's
not much fun.
When we fight
we can't get
anything done.

Hitting hurts,
and screaming irritates.
When we want
to be heard,
we communicate.

We talk it out.
ch ch, ch ch ch
We talk it out
ch, ch, ch ch ch

At times I get
all churning inside.
I don't know
what I feel.
I want to hide.

My day care mom,
she understands.
I'm awful glad
we're in her hands.

I punch a pillow.
ch ch, ch ch ch
I climb a willow.
ch ch, ch ch ch

Other times
I'm able to say,
"I wanna be home,
I don't like it
this way."

I get too tired.
I want my own place.
I need some quiet.
I need some space.

I talk it out.
ch ch, ch ch ch
They hear me out.
ch ch, ch ch ch

But today I'm perky.
I want my friends.
I don't care if day care
ever ends.

We do neat projects
and play a lot.
For fun and activities
this is the spot.

We play it out.
ch ch, ch ch ch
We play it out.
ch ch, ch ch ch
I say it out.
ch ch, ch ch ch
We play it out.
ch ch, ch ch ch
Day care!

Flannelboard Stories

Although it's a handy piece of equipment, you needn't own a 3-foot-square board covered with flannel to make use of flannel stories. A soft baby blanket spread over the back of the couch will do. Early learning supply houses sell pre-cut shapes with story accompaniments, but you can easily make your own flannel pieces. Flannel is a little hard for young children to cut, but they can add to your collection by making paper cut-outs to which you glue a scrap of felt. The felt will hold the paper cut-out to the board or blanket. You can make up characters to illustrate nursery rhymes, or you can make an assortment of shapes to be arranged in patterns or pieced together to make pictures.

For months I was making a new set of characters every few days. I was even beginning to assemble them into flannelboard story packets which I kept in 5 x 7 inch envelopes. Making these sets with the children became an activity in itself.

You must remember, though, that you can't and shouldn't expect yourself to do everything. For a long while now, I haven't even used the flannelboard, let alone made up new characters. You have the freedom to put aside an activity if you've lost your creative connection to it. You can always return to it at a later time. You're able to stay vibrantly alive with the children, well...most of the time anyway.

Use the flannelboard to

- Tell a story.
- Afterwards, let two children at a time retell the same story to the group.
- To teach, as, for example, a sand box story about a misbehaving monster.
- Let the children tell each other stories from your flannel packets.
- Let the children make up new stories by combining sets of pieces.

Play Acting

Pretending, moving, speaking, remembering sequences, and creating good times together, have value themselves. Children have many years ahead for memorizing and reciting.

Young children enjoy acting out short stories and rhymes. However, if you insist on their play becoming a performance, or recording and taking pictures of all they do, you may inhibit their natural inclination towards drama. Pretending, moving, speaking, remembering sequences, and creating good times together, have value themselves. Children have many years ahead for memorizing and reciting. Let play acting at this age be an extension of play; let it be fun.

Plays can be introduced by reading a story. "The Three Bears" and "The Three Billy Goats Gruff" lend themselves beautifully to small group acting. The children can plan what props will be needed as you read, and then let them bring the story to life. Ask questions like: "Will the small slide work for the troll's bridge?" "What pillows can we use for the bears' beds?" This discussion takes the process beyond just acting out the story. The children help plan and problem solve, and the reluctant performers have a safe way to be involved. They can arrange the audience chairs, set out the bears' bowls, or make pretend grass for the goats to eat.

After I've told or read the story and we've "set the stage," I divide the performers into two groups. I like to do two run-throughs, with half the children playing the audience and the other half acting. Then they trade places. This gives the audience a part in the drama and gives you an opportunity to begin educating children in how to be an appreciative and considerate audience.

The following story about unicorns came out of one group's myth. At first I was simply telling it off the top of my head, on one of those magical, harmony-filled mornings when sunbeams shone through a prism on the window sill, sprinkling rainbows all over the room. Later I wrote down the story, and later still we used it for playacting. If "Solaylee and Rubinga" doesn't suit your cast of characters, make up stories that do, using themes and settings that touch your group.

"Solaylee and Rubinga"
by E. Sandy Powell

    Once upon a time, in a time much like now, there lived two unicorns: Solaylee and her little son, Rubinga. They lived up and away over the hills in a rugged forest land.

    What we call "Magic" came easy to Solaylee and Rubinga. They could fly, even though they had no wings. They could make their own food if they had to. And, as long as a sunbeam touched their horns, they could also disappear. Reappearing was very hard work, though, so they didn't disappear often.

    Solaylee and Rubinga's Magic seemed very special. Actually, they weren't really different from the other forest creatures. They had simply figured out what they could do best, being magical unicorns. Then they practiced until they did it well. Doing things well made them feel good about themselves, so they held their heads high and noticed things around them.

    One creature in that forest who didn't feel good about himself was a great old elk named Wannabuck. Instead of thinking of what *he* could do, Wannabuck was always watching Solaylee and Rubinga. He wanted to do Magic, too, but he couldn't. This made him very cross.

One day Wannabuck decided to get rid of Solaylee and Rubinga. He carefully set a snare on the path. But, as Solaylee and Rubinga neared the snare, they started to run faster and faster. Whoop! Zing! They flew into the air, sailing over the sniveling, snarling Wannabuck. Solaylee and Rubinga had sensed the danger just in time.

In the days to follow Wannabuck made other traps, each of them more entangled than the last. But all the traps failed. Wannabuck grew more and more angry. Finally, he grew so angry that he climbed to the top of Mt. Hazard-Worst to get the help of the old hag Grubberwhat.

Grubberwhat stood by her fly-covered caldron, stirring a bubbling brew. She loved making potions for nasty tricks. (Do you know why she liked being nasty? Because nobody had ever loved her. Playing mean tricks was the only way she knew to get attention.)

Wannabuck huffed up behind her.

"Ack!" shrieked Grubberwhat. "What do you want?"

"I want your help," boomed Wannabuck, as soon as he caught his breath. And he told her about the unicorns.

"You're doing it all wrong," she scrabbled. And in a raspy whisper Grubberwhat unraveled a plan. "When you see the pot of gold, you'll know I'm near," she said. Wannabuck bounded back down Mt. Hazard-Worst to make friends with Solaylee and Rubinga, as the old hag had ordered.

On the first day of "The Plan," Wannabuck took Solaylee and Rubinga a fresh Berrywa Pie. On the second day, he worked long and hard making home-made bread and butter. That night, after delivering his gift, he slept fifteen hours. Kindness was a great strain on Wannabuck. During the next four days, he brought them presents until, finally, the seventh day arrived. Solaylee and Rubinga should have known better, but they had actually forgotten how rotten Wannabuck had been. When he asked them to go on a picnic, they said "Yes" right away.

Wannabuck's old knees bungled together as the three of them climbed up the mountain. "Today is the day. The Plan is working," he thought. Only a small doubt crept through his mind. Maybe he'd have more fun just being friends. But he swished the doubt away, for his old heart hadn't yet opened.

When at last they reached the wildflower meadow, Solaylee became uneasy. A perfect rainbow arched over the picnic ground, and Rubinga ran ahead. But something didn't feel right to Solaylee, so she raced to reach her little one. She caught up with him just as he stopped by the pot of gold.

Before Solaylee could warn Rubinga, the lid spun off. Grubberwhat leapt from a nearby bush and shoved them into the pot, kerbang!

"A'crack! A'cren!
Oh, Whoopee!
Never again
Will you be free!"
cackled the jealous old hag. Wannabuck chugged up to the pot of gold. He felt glad, everywhere that is but deep in his thick old chest.

From within a tiny flower, a faint fluttering could be heard. But Wannabuck and Grubberwhat were too busy applauding themselves to pay attention to the world around them. As they lumbered down the mountain path, a baby fairy flew out of the flower and landed on the pot of gold.

(Of course you know that a spell can be broken if another spell is chanted before the rainbow disappears.)

Quickly, in his high baby voice, the fairy sang:
"Trillium trum,
You will see.
When the children come,
You will be free."

The tiny fairy had never cast a spell before. As the rainbow faded away, he wished he'd cast up a different one. What if the children never came! Feeling responsible, the little fairy stayed right there to watch over the unicorns. Nights and days and several moons passed, and still Solaylee and Rubinga were trapped inside the pot of gold. The little fairy finally decided to go find some children, for he didn't want to spend his whole life there, waiting.

Off he went, hopping through the woods, sliding down the waterfalls and flying through the valley until he came to a fine town. And there, of course, he found many children who were eager to help. On the way back to the meadow, the little fairy taught them this song:

Come with me, now you're free, So-lay-lee and Ru-bin-ga.

Come with me, now you're free, So-lay-lee and Ru-bin-ga.

Rounding Out Your Program 105

When the children and the fairy got to the pot of gold and sang in their clear cool voices, the lid creaked open, and Solaylee and Rubinga were free.

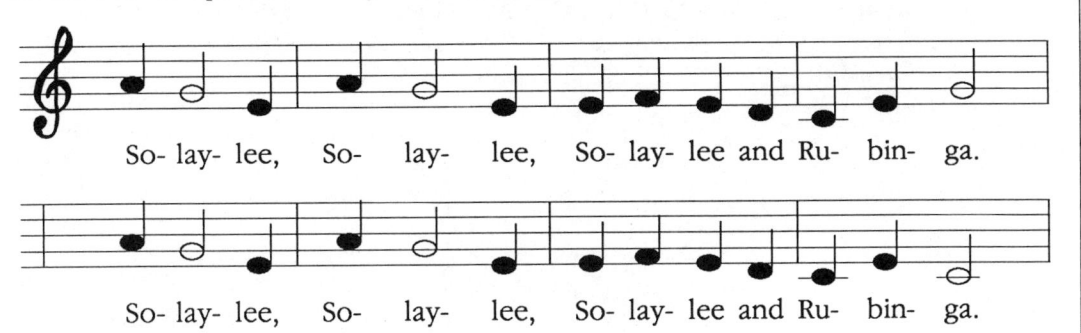

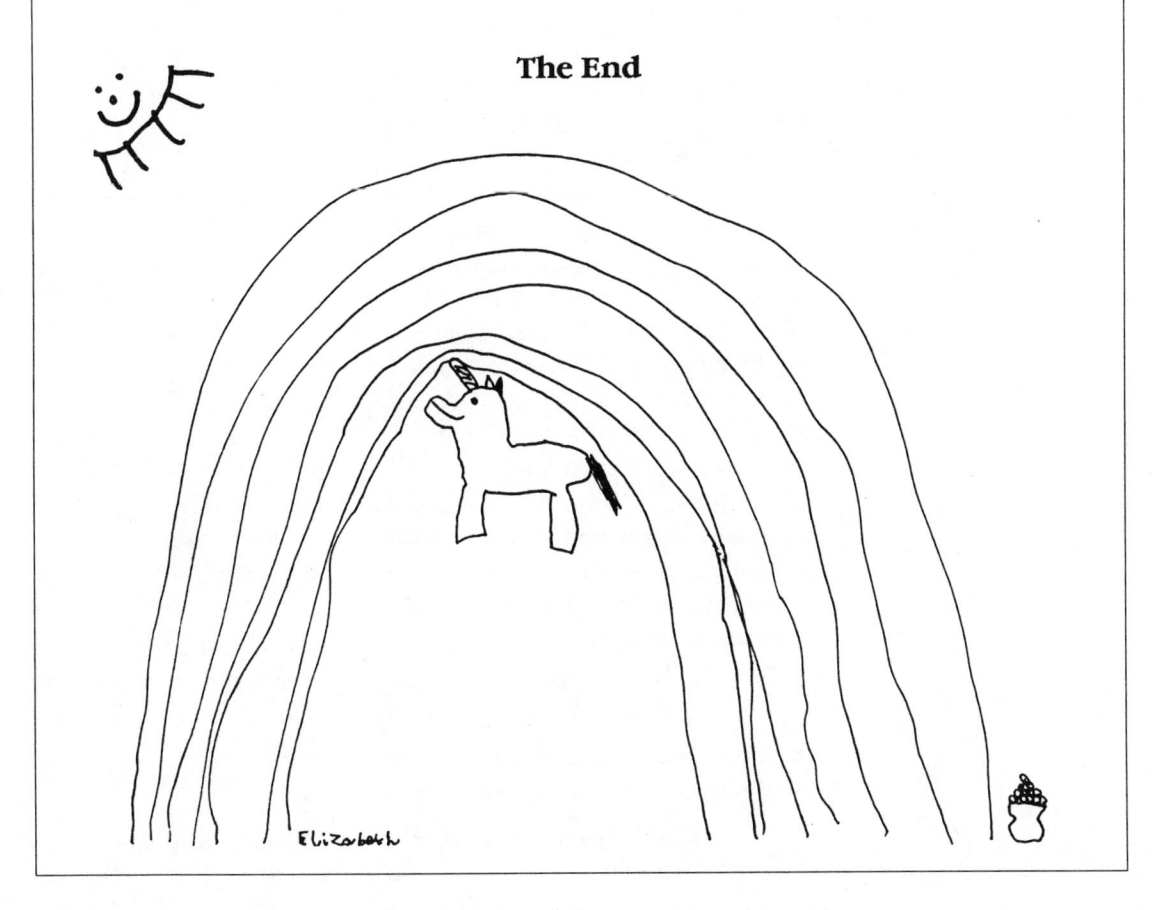

So- lay- lee, So- lay- lee, So- lay- lee and Ru- bin- ga.

So- lay- lee, So- lay- lee, So- lay- lee and Ru- bin- ga.

The End

Storytelling

As with the activities described earlier, begin with what you know best.

You can join librarians and school teachers who are bringing back the lost art of storytelling. Very simple stories told by you can spark imaginations dulled by too much TV. You needn't be an orator, actress, or even particularly imaginative at first. The only quality you really need is a willingness to try.

As with the activities described earlier, begin with what you know best. Tell the children stories

- of your childhood
- of your parents' or grandparents' growing up
- of the funniest thing you ever did
  - the scariest
  - the hardest
  - the most embarrassing

Encourage the children to take turns listening and telling each other their "Most" stories. You may have to gently limit the time as, once they have an audience, some children will go on and on. Reassure them with a plan for the next day's storytelling.

Anticipate tall tales told from the need to impress. For initial storytelling exercises, focus less on the issue of truth and more on the fun in communicating. Using your stories as examples, encourage the children to identify the stories as made-up or true. The short-storytelling time *will* foster exaggeration. If you're having difficulty with a child lying, deal with it straightforwardly with the child and parent(s), at a separate time. Sometimes story time can be offered to a child who is prone to lying, as a set time when he/she has permission to let their imagination take over. You can guide the child to identify the story with "This is my tall tale."

If you're not comfortable spinning a yarn, remember you're storytelling to *children*. Perhaps by nurturing a shy child's courage now, you can help alleviate your kind of stage fright for that child later on. Here are a few ideas to help you feel at ease:

- Use your hands and arms, stand up, move around, or run in place if you need to to make a point.
- While you're telling the story, picture the place you're talking about, and simply describe what you see.
- When describing the setting, start at the top and move to the bottom, or start in the foreground and move to the background.

Rounding Out Your Program 107

If you plan your story ahead of time, you can fashion a descriptive phrase that rolls off the tongue, one to repeat every time you mention a main character, such as, "The dog with big paws, curly hair, and one brown ear flopped down."

This helps the children move with you in their mind's eyes.

- Repeat phrases, colors, or identifying characteristics. Say, for example, "When I went to Auntie's house I opened the gate, skipped up the walk, and rapped the little door knocker." The children will soon be finishing the repeated line each time you set it in motion. If you plan your story ahead of time, you can fashion a descriptive phrase that rolls off the tongue, one to repeat every time you mention a main character, such as, "The dog with big paws, curly hair, and one brown ear flopped down." If every time you say "the dog," you begin "the dog with..." the children will love finishing the sentence for you.

- Allow yourself to insert silly rhymes into your story like "The dog curled up by a log in the fog." Or alliterate excessively: "Leela Langley lost her lamb." You'll be encouraging fun with language that will carry over to the children's creative writing later on.

Finally, after telling lots of stories from your experience, try some simple make-believe stories. Watch the children's faces as you use their names in the story. You might begin: "Once upon a time, Cynthia, Jack, and Aaron (...your children's names) wanted to ride in a balloon. They walked out to farmer Della's field and paid her the $2 each for the ride. Della boosted Cynthia, Jack, and Aaron up into the basket. While she was getting ready for lift off, the lead rope slipped loose. The children tried to pull Della up, but they couldn't. Della had to let go of the rope and jump to safety. Aaron called to her for instructions. But the wind quickly took them away. Up, up they went...."

Your children can help tell the ending. What happened to the children? Where did they go? How did they get down? How did they get home again? Let the children answer questions like these a bit at a time. Then use their suggestions to go on with the story.

Continue this kind of storytelling experiment, and, you'll have yet another 20 to 30 minute quiet activity to schedule into your week. I think you'll be pleased at how much these short, structured times affect the quality of your caregiving. The following "Pterodactyls in the Garden" came out of one such ad-libbing story time with four and five-year-olds.

"Pterodactyls in the Garden"
by E. Sandy Powell

Once upon a time, away off over the hills, past Somewhere Else and down, a family of pterodactyls lived in a creaky old castle. Vines covered the castle turrets and trailed onto the ground. All winter long the pterodactyls slept, wrapped in feathers on the cold stone floors.

But every spring the pterodactyls woke up, cawed and screeched, creaked open the massive doors, and flew out of their castle walls, up and away past Somewhere Else and over the hills to the village. The villagers didn't have much money, but they were happy just the same because of all the lovely flowers they grew. Even the children loved to grow flowers. But every spring those pesky pterodactyls swooped into town, and yanked up the daffodils, the crocuses, and the tulips. Away they would fly with flowers trailing from their beaks, away off over the hills, past Somewhere Else and down to their own cold castle. Every spring for 17 years, they had raided the flowers.

When the pterodactyls arrived back home, they creaked open their castle door—SQUEAK!—clamored down the cellar stairs—TROMP Fluffel TROMP Fluffel!—and opened the dungeon door—CREAK, CREAK! Onto a mighty, cold, moldy pile they threw the village flowers. "Caw, caw, caw!" the pterodactyls shrieked as they slammed the door—BAM!—and laughed their way up, up, up the stairs.

Rounding Out Your Program 109

When summer came, the pterodactyls ventured out once more. They cawed and screeched, creaked open the massive doors, and flew out of their castle walls, up and away past Somewhere Else, over the hills to the village. This time they swooped down to yank up the sweet peas, the zinnias, and the petunias. "Caw, caw, caw!" they shrieked as the children screamed and fumed. But the pterodactyls, flowers trailing from their beaks, flew away off over the hills, past Somewhere Else and down to their own cold castle.

Arriving home they creaked open the castle door—SQUEAK!—clamored down the cellar stairs—TROMP Fluffel, TROMP Fluffel!—opened the dungeon door—CREAK, CREAK!—and onto a mighty, cold, moldy pile they threw the village flowers.

Well, the children of the village had had quite enough of the flower snatching thieves. Without telling their mothers or fathers, they sneaked out of their beds that night, packed up their sacks with sweet nuts and minced treats, and headed away off over the hills past Somewhere Else and down, through the thorns and vines, to the pterodactyls' cold castle.

"Knock, knock, knock!" pounded the brave, brave children.

"Caw, caw, caw!" shrieked the pterodactyls.

"Run, run, run!" thought the children. But a brave spot within each of them made the children stay strong.

CREAK!—they opened the massive doors. "Caw, caw, caw!" echoed the pterodactyls.

And the little children, shivering in their shoes, simply asked, "Why?"

"Have you come to fight?" screamed the birds.

"No, we don't want to fight," said the children. "We just want to know why. Why do you take our flowers every year?"

"Ho, Ho!" screamed the pterodactyls. "Why do you think? Because we don't have any flowers of our own."

"That's right. No flowers. No poor pterodactyls' flowers," fluttered all the birds. "Poor, poor birdies."

The children looked at each other, an idea awakening in their heads.

"Wait right here!" they called to the pterodactyls, as they ran out of the castle thorns, up and away past Somewhere Else, and over the hills to the village.

This time they packed their sacks with seeds and roped on shovels, rakes, and hoes. The littlest carried her Granny's old leaky watering can. Away off over the hills they went, past Somewhere Else and down, to the thorny castle.

Straightaway they cleared the vines. They didn't even shiver at the pterodactyls' screeching.

Dig and dig and dig and dig, and dig and dig and dig went the shovels.

Hoe and hoe and hoe and hoe, and hoe and hoe and hoe followed the hoes.

Somebody called out, "Let's make it smooth!"

> So rake and rake and rake and rake, and rake and rake and rake they went. "Now for the seeds!"
> Plant and plant and plant and plant, and plant and plant and plant.
> Then pat and pat and pat and pat, and pat and pat and pat.
> Next they staked off the garden plot and called to the pterodactyls. The youngest and most forgiving of the children handed Granny's leaky watering can to the oldest and most gnarly bird. "Just keep them moist and they'll grow," she said.
> "Yay! Yay! Yay!" they all yelled, children and pterodactyls together.
> And from that summer on, both the children and pterodactyls grew flowers. At least once a season they went, away off, over the hills, past Somewhere Else and on to visit each other's gardens. They traded their most colorful and sweetest smelling flowers, and happy were they all.
> Caw! Caw!
>
> **The End**

When I tell "Pterodactyls in the Garden," the children help make the sound effects and motions, including a wavy hand path in front of them that dips down each time the story passes Somewhere Else on the way to the castle. As you can see, the repetition, the rhythms, and the motions are what make a story. Try telling your own, and encourage the children to help you. And, most of all, have fun!

Holidays

As the years go by, I yield more and more major holiday traditions to the families. I don't make a month-long event out of Christmas, Hanukkah, and Easter as I used to, and I try to keep Halloween and Valentine hype to a minimum. Greens and trees and hiding eggs belong to families. As children spend more of their time away from home, families lose time for and touch with their own traditions. I've even heard little ones complain, "But we already carved pumpkins at day care; do we have to do it again?" Parents deserve the primary involvement, particularly for religious holidays. You can help foster acceptance and appreciation by having a special sharing time for each child to show and tell how his/her family celebrates its special holidays.

As children spend more of their time away from home, families lose time for and touch with their own traditions. I've even heard little ones complain, "But we already carved pumpkins at day care; do we have to do it again?"

You can refrain from adding to the sugar-filled parties and seasonal treats. Children can't help but be out of control with non-stop intake of sugar. One of the best gifts I can give children, during the holidays is the chance to be healthy and rested. So, I try to stay calm and help the children stay calm, offering a few select projects and outings.

Our activities at Christmas and Hanukkah center around giving. We give our songs, decorate trees outdoors for the birds, and give food to people who don't have enough. We might also bake cookies, make red and green paintings, or do whatever seems appropriate for the children that year, but only as it nourishes them, not just because it's expected. I'll easily scrap a holiday plan if the children are too tired. They might just need to play alone or curl up on my lap for a story. As we set out on one "giving" expedition, I was tempted to cancel for my sake. We'd planned a trip to the nursing home. Since all that year's families celebrated Christmas, we'd practiced a few simple carols to sing for the residents. Bundled up, with bells ringing, we headed out to the van.

The morning was exceptionally cold. My gloveless fingers were freezing as I struggled, adjusting seat belts. With one-year-olds, there were also the car seats to wrestle with. This particular morning I was barely able to manage it all. The children were pushing each other, and the windows all needed the ice scraped off. I wondered, not for the first time, why I bothered with enriching activities.

But I was so pleased once we got there. The children visited Aunt Marge in her room and wanted to visit others as well. And, yes, we even sang and jingled bells for a whole group of seniors. The hearts of the residents were lightened at the sight of those little ones, and the children still talk about that trip. I must take them more often, year round.

Another time we went to the grocery store to buy canned goods that we delivered to the fire station. An excerpt from my note home to parents will give you a feeling for this holiday giving.

Dec. 13

Dear —

The magic of this season and the love potential in ongoing togetherness has once again enveloped our little world. Yes, the children are tired and excited, so wills and heads have collided more frequently than usual. But even on a Friday the ho, ho, ho's keep bubbling out and I've been able to laugh the children out of most conflicts. Today, along with the crotcheties, I heard so much caring: "I like you," "I like what you're wearing today," and "Thank you," among themselves.

And, oh, what pleasure we had in our shopping trip. Once inside the store, the children looked and pointed, mulling over what people who don't have much food might want. After quite some debate and a little changing of minds ("No, they won't want two cans of peas!" each child settled on an item, which they purchased, one by one. Then we drove to the fire station, the cans clutched tightly in their arms. A perfect gentle fireman escorted us into the collection room. We lifted the children up so they could deposit their cans in the big barrels themselves. The fireman opened the station doors so we could walk out past the big engines.

On our way home we drove through town to "ooh's" and "ahh's" over the lights and Santa pictures....

♡
Sand

Many holidays focus on religious events. Unless a caregiver advertises herself/himself as a member of a particular faith (in which case the parents are paying for a certain ideology as well as child care), spiritual education should be left with the families. I have very strong beliefs myself. Knowing how malleable young minds are, I would feel uncomfortable trying to influence them to think as I do. I prefer trying to live what I believe, perhaps a more powerful influence anyway, and leave religious discussion and instruction in the homes. This way I am free to care for children of any religion, and I can continue to feel ethical about my relationship with the families.

Rounding Out Your Program

I often select and invent our own holidays, and I can choose times that suit us, times that add to, rather than take away from, a family's holiday celebration.

Holidays offer a unique opportunity to bring a group together, to savor life specially, to warm a cold spell, or to brighten a long rainy season. I often select and invent our own holidays, and I can choose times that suit us, times that add to, rather than take away from, a family's holiday celebration.

Teddy Bear Day

Some great holiday traditions arise from a set of negative circumstances. That's how "Teddy Bear Day" got started. A heavy snowfall had cut short festivities before winter break. When we got back together, I think I still felt guilty about the abrupt ending to the last year. I know I also had post-holiday, winter let-down. We were listening to a new Teddy Bear record when I thought, "'Teddy Bear Day!' Let's make a holiday! Each child could bring his or her own teddy bear". And they did! This is the note I wrote home after the first Teddy Bear Day.

Dear Everybody,

This has got to be a carboned note today. I'm exhausted!

I was delighted to see so many bears show up today and especially tickled to see P— walk in with a four-foot tall one. As the first hour wore on, though, that big bear grew, in my mind at least, until he was a good eight feet high, with power to match. But more of big bear in a minute.

The boys and E— began their day with....you guessed it, Teddy Bear pancakes. Raisins for faces added a touch we hadn't tried before. Then I passed out receiving blankets. The girls arrived and got theirs, too, along with a teddy bear stamp on everyone's hands.

We had planned a quiet little tea. (I'm sure the quiet was my idea.)...but that big bear! He just couldn't control himself and had the children rolling and punching and bouncing all over. He nearly received the first exception to my no spanking policy (on the bear, not the child). As you know, "time out" is my last resort. Poor big bear suffered greatly out in the van, all by himself. (Caused Grandma Kay quite a start, too, to see him at the wheel when she stopped by.)

The rest of the morning proceeded fine with groups of children serving bears Cheerios in the china tea set. They also rocked and read to their bears and dressed them in all sorts of clothes. We had only a very little fighting over bears. They were all really quite gracious.

And, yes, some of us danced to "Me and My Teddy Bear" and heard other teddy bear songs. Gummy bears surprised the children at snacks, just a few to go with bananas and milk. And big bear finally earned the right to return.

At this moment six bears and six children are sleeping soundly. I must go. I promised teddy bear outlines to color when they wake up. Bye!

♡
Sand

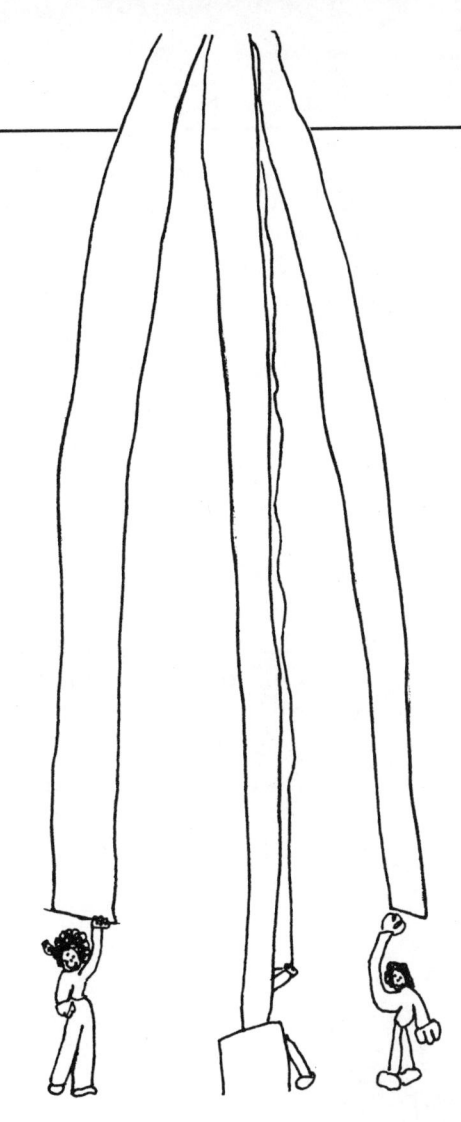

May Day

May Day's a perfect children's holiday, and I try to celebrate it every year. Because most people don't celebrate it anymore, it's much appreciated by the parents, older neighbors, and children.

First we make and decorate the May baskets. Next, we fill the baskets with flowers from our yard and then carry our baskets on a walk around the neighborhood. Two by two, the children go up to a door. They hang a basket on the doorknob, ring the bell, and run back to the rest of us waiting at the curb. The children love the challenge of getting away uncaught. Most years we make an extra basket to drive down to the nursing home.

After the baskets, we have the May Pole. Outdoors or in, I always try to have a pole, topped with balloons, ready with crepe paper to wind round and round. Traditionally the children weave over and under each other, but my groups have always been too young, so we just go round and round. Usually the May song is something I make up on the spot, because I never can remember the proper tune.

Then we have the treats. I would be pleased to report little May cakes all wrapped in pretty papers. I do get something special, but it's usually bakery-made, flower-shaped cookies. Most children have never had a May Day, so whatever you do is a treat.

Washington's Birthday

Another favorite winter holiday is Washington's birthday. That is the gardener's superstition day: "Plant your peas on Washington's birthday (traditional date, of course) and you'll have a good crop." Well, that won't work for many of you who are thoroughly snowed in on February 22. But in our northwest climate, Washington's birthday is perfect for peas, cooped-up caregivers, and children.

Here's how the day goes: We have already turned the soil two weeks before. We've added manure or mulch, worked it in, and then let the ground rest. By Washington's birthday, we are out taking turns smoothing the dirt. We plant sweet peas because I love the beautiful fragrant multi-colored flowers just right for a somewhat protected southern exposure.

I soak the peas the night before. Each child gets a small handful. One by one we go down a row, poking and patting our seeds. One year I had the children paint stakes in rainbow colors, and we pounded them in around the border after our planting. Then we all lined up to sing "Happy Growing To You."

Weather permitting, we end our holiday on a blanket next to the garden plot. Usually late February is awash with sun, perfect for an unseasonal picnic of nuts and oranges, or maybe cocoa if it's still nippy.

Election Day

I'm grateful to the Camas Public School Kindergarten Team for adding November 8, voting day, to my calendar. I've always celebrated our right to vote with my own children, but the kindergarten teachers and aides gave me activity ideas suitable for preschoolers.

Children are never too young to practice the caring and responsibility required of voters, and what better way than to present the responsibility as a right to be treasured.

Children are never too young to practice the caring and responsibility required of voters, and what better way than to present the responsibility as a right to be treasured. Elections should be a festive time, because we have choices. Here are some activities you can offer your children that allow them to celebrate their right to vote.

- Ahead of time, type up 3 x 5 inch Voter Registration cards.

> **VOTER REGISTRATION**
> This is to certify that
> _Elisha T._
> is registered to vote.

Children old enough to write can sign or initial their cards.

- Have everyone make VOTE badges. Cut circles out of white paper. The children can color their own and tape on red and blue crepe paper tails.

Rounding Out Your Program 117

- Make up a list of your children. Compile the list in a simple two-page Voter's Registration.
- Wearing their VOTE badges and carrying their Voter Registration cards, the children go to your designated Polling Place. They must show their Voter's Registration card and sign the register alongside their name (with their signature, their initials, or an X).
- If it's a presidential election, you can have pictures posted of the two top runners, color coded onto the ballots. Or you can pick an issue that will impact your families.
- Let the children mark their ballots for one candidate/issue or another.
- Have the children place their ballots in a sealed ballot box.
- After the polls are "closed," take out the ballots and tally them on a simple graph. Have the children help you color in who "won" the election.
- Be sure to stress our right to different points of view. "Put-downs" aren't allowed.
- Have red, white, and blue frosted cake or cookies, or red delicious apples, blueberries and milk for your voting day snacks.

As home day care providers we have another freedom: making up our own holidays.

Ground Hog Day, Feb. 2; **Arbor Day**, the date varies, often the last Friday in April; and **Flag Day**, June 14, are other traditional holidays you can celebrate. As home day care providers we have another freedom: making up our own holidays. Try having a "Unicorny," or a "Mary Poppins Holiday" for a change. Suit the special days to your children, your weather, and your personal needs.

Don't bother to be bound by a prescribed schedule. A few years ago I pulled my back out lifting little ones just before May Day. I never mentioned the holiday because I could barely get around, much less put up and supervise a May pole. I knew the older brother of two little ones I cared for would notice the absence of a May pole, since he'd so thoroughly appreciated our May Day the year previous. But the holiday was never really missed in our group, and I was free to celebrate the next year with renewed gusto.

Chapter 6
Taking Care of Yourself

In spite of the major hardships, home caregiving is one of the most honorable and needed professions available.

I've been to the bottom of my heart over the question: Why be a child caregiver? In spite of the major hardships, home caregiving is one of the most honorable and needed professions available. Opportunities for serving humankind are at every door. But, I'm convinced, we could travel the world over and not find a greater need than child caring. Thousands and thousands of young American children leave home every day because their parent(s) work. Actually, the figure is in the millions; I find millions hard to fathom, and more parents join the work force every day. More children become "working children." These children have a right to be nurtured and cared for.

Some little ones do fine in a day care setting. Day care centers can provide for the total well-being of the child, but most centers can't provide the relaxed care found in home day care. Parents have home day care and larger day care centers to choose between. No

Children deserve to be loved and nurtured every day. As a home child caregiver, you can offer your unique type of nurturing to children that need it.

one type of care is right for everybody. All children, however, will have to relate to the lack of mother/father physical closeness during the workday. Children need this love, not just from 6 to 7 a.m. and 5 to 7 p.m., but all day, every day. Someone has to give to them, hold them, guide them, care for them. Growing up isn't easy, but it can include delight, laughter, purposeful work, and delicious play. That kind of childhood begins with a committed adult.

When I tried to meet the needs of five or six young children, 40 to 50 hours a week, plus meet the needs of their families as they overlapped with our home day care, while parenting my own three children, I risked ballooning into Mammoth Mother—here for everybody, hearing everybody, giving to everyone, and never stopping to listen to *me*. How are you doing, Sandy? What do you need? Or, as my little Elizabeth puts it, "What can I do for ya, Mommy?" I should have been asking myself that question. I didn't, and I ended up sick and needing a major operation, one that sapped my stamina and good health. I even had to quit caregiving for almost two years.

You can't give, give, give without getting revived, rejuvenated, and renourished from time to time. You can't stay tuned to the needs of others without paying attention to your own needs, or eventually you'll pay the price. The outcome will surely be ill health or ill temper.

Self Awareness and Acceptance

I need to be in touch with myself. I need to listen to my throbbing tooth, for instance. The ache may be a cavity calling out for repair, but this time the ache is from tension. I'm not relaxed, I'm tense and jittery from afternoon coffee. I've been clenching my jaw for an hour. So, naturally, I have a tooth ache. Time out: 3 minutes of facial relaxation exercises, and I feel better. It's as simple as that. As a caregiver, you need to be self aware and then do some little act for yourself at the moment of need.

How many times during a day care year do I get oh-so-tired? How many times do I either need lots of orange juice and rest to ward off a cold, or an evening bike ride to enliven my unconditioned body, or the words of an inspiring book to spark my atrophied mind? Oh, so often!

The trick for me is to stay aware, pay attention, tune in to what's going on inside, and then do one little thing. Ordinarily I might become aware, but I tell myself I shouldn't be gaining weight, or getting tired, or feeling ill. I don't accept what I know, and I don't do anything in response to the original awareness. This three minutes of relaxing *did help.* A bike ride over to the school *has helped.* A half hour alone *does help.* The main thing is to be aware of my imbalance and to brainstorm what I can do to make it better. The solution isn't in the whole picture: the children, their families, my own children, the house, the yard, etc. The solution for imbalance is inside me. What would help me right now? Sometimes cleaning the kitchen counter *would* really help, but I need to be sure that I'm not just heaping up more on the Mammoth Mother. Self awareness gives me an opportunity to accept myself.

I am just now learning to accept my rhythms. I have high and low energy parts of the day. I don't try to do much, for instance, between 3:30 and 5:00 p.m., when I'm almost without energy. I have to relax and recharge. Since I know that about myself, I can schedule my time so I don't have big demands in the late afternoon. After all, I've been up and going strong since 6 a.m., and I won't be finished and in bed until 11:30 p.m. or midnight. It doesn't matter who among us wins the martyr's award for working longer and harder. It matters that each of us knows when and how long to work and when to slow down and rest. We are all different, but none of us can go through life at full speed all the time.

I need to learn to accept times of greater stress, too, or times when I'm working through a problem or helping a friend or family member. I'm not super-human. Sometimes I might rise to the occasion and have an incredible week with the children, in spite of the extra demands. It's more likely that I'll have a tougher time until I get through the difficulty. I also have my faults, my aggravating idiosyncrasies, my short-comings. These must be accepted, too.

> *It matters that each of us knows when and how long to work and when to slow down and rest. We are all different, but none of us can go through life at full speed all the time.*

Doing Something Is Better Than Doing Nothing At All

List of Loves

One caring-for-myself measure is to keep a "List of Loves" on the bulletin board or some other visible spot. As a preventative step, I treat myself to one of those loves every week. If I've slipped a little in caring for myself or let the demands crowd in and overwhelm me, I don't have to *think*, I just have to *do* one in order to feel better.

My list includes:
- taking a walk
- buying some honey roasted peanuts
- browsing in my favorite store downtown
- calling a good friend long distance
- writing a letter (A chore for some people, letter writing nurtures me as I allow myself time to be in touch with friends.)
- riding my bike
- driving to the ocean (reserved for every few months), etc.

Your list of loves will be different, a unique reflection of you.

Caregiving can be an overwhelming job. But by making a commitment to yourself to do some self-care, you can continue to thrive as a caregiver.

Assessing Limitations

Some of my limitations have been:

- The number of children I care for, usually six full-time, including my own daughter.
- The ages of the children I care for, no more than two under the age of two.
- The year before my operation I had to add another limitation. I realized I needed that half hour when everyone is sleeping, just for me. Even the half hour is never guaranteed: baby might be fussy, or a child might have trouble getting to sleep. My need for even a very short break meant I couldn't enroll kindergartners. That was a particularly difficult decision because it meant losing one of my main families whose oldest child was no longer napping. At that time I was just beginning to learn that, first of all, I have to take care of me.

Other limitations:

- Whether children are potty trained or in diapers, ambulatory children or babies needing to be carried, bottle babies or children who feed themselves. I have strained my back enough that I've thought I should only enroll petite babies, but I never have accepted that limitation. These considerations all determine whom I will care for and how I will feel year-round.

Making Agreements

Next, I have to make arrangements and agreements with the parents to prevent caregiver burnout. I have to be aware of what my needs are, and of how I can arrange my work so that I am able to continue giving quality care. Then I have to assert those needs to the parents. For instance, I decided long ago to have the children bring their own lunches. I'd rather spend my time and energy providing activities than cooking casseroles. You might find it easier to do both; cooking doesn't come easily to me.

Some of my hardest moments in home child care have been in asserting my needs. I've had to turn away a third child in diapers, or turn away a family I really wanted to work with because combining our work schedules meant I'd have eleven-hour days. I know that to continue the kind of activities and program outlined in this book, I need separate time for my family and at least a little time for myself.

Next, I have to make arrangements and agreements with the parents to prevent caregiver burnout. I have to be aware of what my needs are, and of how I can arrange my work so that I am able to continue giving quality care.

What an opportunity we have, to be able to create our own best working environments! Most jobs don't offer such freedom.

Making Changes

Another way to care for myself is to alter my responsibilities. If I can see that I'm getting overly tired or perhaps just lonely for other adults, I can hire a helper for half a day a week. I might prefer, like one caregiver I know, to take the afternoon off and have the adult substitute. Or I might wish to "team teach" on that afternoon, planning activities, field trips, or events that work better with more than one adult. Another person's perspective with your children can be enlightening and can give you fresh insights that will help you the rest of the week. I've benefited so much from occasional help from my parents or friends. Scheduling this on a regular basis would be even better. By accepting what I have to offer, my style, and my limitations (i.e. my whole self), I am a clearer and happier person, more able to care for the children.

Sometimes parents can present problems. While many of your parents will have come to grips with their complex roles as working parents, others will remain overwhelmed with guilt. On the surface they are glad that their child is so happy with you, but they may feel confused by their child's attachment to you and threatened by your care. We get to spend 8 to 10 hours a day exclusively with their children while they spend only a few hours a day together. They need to juggle household maintenance, shopping, and cooking along with their parenting. It's no wonder that some come to resent the wonderful day care home that they sought out for their child. In a case like that, the only thing you can do is your best to care for their child. And take care of yourself.

Giving Yourself Credit

Finally, give yourself credit for the quality of your caregiving. When you offer a month of experimenting, cooking projects, periodic "messy" projects, field trips, special day care holidays, plus ongoing guidance in the children's social, physical, mental, and emotional development; when you read stacks of books in a year, write even some notes home to the parents, hold, rock and cuddle their children, dance with them and exercise to enthusiastic aerobics (the list goes on and on), you are giving wonderful care! Remember to give yourself credit, pat yourself on the back, and treat yourself when you're doing well. You deserve it.

Another person's perspective with your children can be enlightening and can give you fresh insights that will help you the rest of the week. I've benefited so much from occasional help from my parents or friends.

If this is a time when you're not doing any of those things, when you're really not doing a great job, still be gentle with yourself. Don't beat yourself down further. Do just one little thing like turn off the TV and take the children for a walk around the block. Do one little thing for you and the children, and then remember to give yourself credit for it. You'll feel better and so will they.

I often think how lucky I am to have my three children, to live with and grow with. (I remind myself of that when I'm worrying about my older two being out late or when I'm trying to reach the toothpaste over all the paraphernalia on the bathroom counter!) I'm an essential part of my children's lives, and we're bound together, interdependent. The children in my day care home, though, will grow up with or without my care. So when parents choose me, especially when I connect with their children, when we have fun, and, yes, even experience "the magic" together, then I am lucky all over again.

A moment, a day, a year of happiness with children is a real gift. Treasure it.

A moment, a day, a year of happiness with children is a real gift. Treasure it. And remember to be good to yourself, so that you can continue to give your rich and joyful care. "Working children" need caregivers like you.

Other Helpful Publications From Toys 'n Things Press:

All Season Fun & Frolic — Indoor and outdoor activities for toddlers to school age.

Basic Guide to Family Day Care Record Keeping — Clear instructions on keeping necessary family day care business records.

Calendar-Keeper — Activities, family day care record keeping, recipes and more. Updated annually. Most popular publication in the field.

Child Care Resource & Referral Counselors & Trainers Manual — Both a ready reference for the busy phone counselor and a training guide for resource and referral agencies.

The Dynamic Infant — Combines an overview of child development with innovative movement and sensory experiences for infants and toddlers.

Family Day Caring magazine — The best source of information on every aspect of home-based child care.

Family Day Care Tax Workbook — Updated every year, latest step-by-step information on forms, depreciation, etc.

For You, For Them — Trainer bibliography of audio-visual and print resources in 6 topic areas.

Forms Kit for Directors — Over 150 reproducible forms covering every need in an early childhood program.

Kids Encyclopedia of Things to Make and Do — Nearly 2,000 art and craft projects for children aged 4-10.

Open the Door, Let's Explore — Full of fun, inexpensive neighborhood walks and field trips designed to help young children.

S.O.S. Kit for Directors — Offers range of brainstormed solutions to everyday questions and problems.

Sharing in the Caring — Packets with family day care parent brochure, contracts and hints.

Staff Orientation in Early Childhood Programs — Complete manual for orienting new staff on all program areas.

Survival Kit for Early Childhood Directors — Solutions, implementation steps and results to handling difficulties with children, staff, parents.

Teachables From Trashables — Step-by-step guide to making over 50 fun toys from recycled household junk.

Teachables II — Similar to above; with another 75-plus toys.

Those Mean Nasty Dirty Downright Disgusting but... Invisible Germs — A delightful story that reinforces for children the benefits of frequent hand washing.